CONTENTS

Foreword v

Introduction vi

The Author 1

Synopsis 3

Chapter Studies

    Chapter One 5

    Chapter Two 13

    Chapter Three 18

    Chapter Four 24

    Chapter Five 28

    Chapter Six 37

    Chapter Seven 44

    Chapter Eight 50

    Chapter Nine 58

    Chapter Ten 64

Characters 75

Interpretation 113

Themes 118

Literary Features 126

The Examination 131

Historical References 164

For the Advanced Student 173

Select Bibliography 182

STUDENTS' GUIDE

TO

ANIMAL FARM

Martin King

Tynron Press

© Martin King, 1989

First published in 1989 by
Tynron Press
Thornhill
Dumfriesshire DG3 4LD
Scotland

ISBN <u>1-871948</u>-08-8

Reprinted 1990, 1991

Illustrations by Tan Bak Leng
Cover design by Eric Yeo
Typeset by Lolitho (Pte) Ltd
Printed in Singapore by Ocean Colour Printing

FOREWORD

This guidebook is aimed primarily at the 'O' level student, but it is hoped that 'N' level students, and teachers, might also find parts of it useful. I believe that it is best to look on the study of literature as an enjoyable exercise, giving you time to reflect on your own life, and the world as others see it. Progressively more challenging books to study mean that you need help, and the best way is by some systematically organised discussion — either in class, or with friends. That is why I have supplied many questions, to help you to recognise the important points, and to provide you with a framework for discussing your response to them.

At this point, on a more personal note, I should like to thank Joyce for all the effort she so generously put into typing the manuscript for *Students' Guide to Animal Farm*, and Ratna for the help with the glossary and background.

Martin King
1989

N.B. All page references are to the Penguin edition of the text.

INTRODUCTION

Animal Farm is a very easy book to read. It offers much important insight into human nature, and it seems to say that there will always be the strong to exploit the weak, and that nothing really changes or improves. This is something for you to discuss and decide for yourselves.

The other big problem is that most teenagers, and not a few adults, are bored by politics and history. Orwell realised this, so instead of writing a newspaper article which would be like a dull sermon, he presented modern history in a very light and amusing manner, and in this way his grim message reached millions of readers.

I have included a lot of background material on history and politics. I hope you are not put off by this, but realise that it is necessary for a deeper understanding of the book.

The central concept of *Animal Farm* is simple. Orwell saw a little boy in Wallington, the village where he once lived, "whipping a huge carthorse along a narrow path." It struck him that "if only such animals became aware of their strength we should have no power over them, and that men exploit animals in much the same way as the rich exploit the proletariat" (the workers).

This small incident, and the reflections it provoked, led to the writing of a book that has been translated into numerous languages and read by millions of people.

THE AUTHOR

George Orwell's real name was Eric Blair. Born in India in 1903, he became a poor "scholarship boy" in a snobbish, ill-run English prep school. The horrors of his schooldays live in a bitter essay, "Such, Such Were the Joys". He did, however, win a scholarship to Eton.

Unwilling to face university life and further snobbery, Orwell went to Burma in 1921, where he spent five years as a policeman and wrote his first novel, *Burmese Days*. Disgusted by his first-hand glimpse of imperialism, Orwell quit his job and went to live in Paris and London, subsisting on infrequent, squalid jobs in restaurant kitchens. His experiences led him to the writing of his first great book, *Down and Out in Paris and London* (1933).

From then on Orwell struggled to earn a living as a journalist and author. He became involved in various left-wing causes during the depression but always remained suspicious of any political doctrine when it violated the basic human rights of the individual. Political idealism led him to fight on the Loyalist side in the Spanish Civil War, in which he was wounded. Returning to England, he wrote *Homage to Catalonia,* an impassioned attack on the betrayal of the Spanish Loyalists by the Communists. Orwell's blistering contempt for the police states he saw growing in Spain, Italy, Germany, and Russia, combined with his warnings to England of the imminent conflict between democracy and totalitarianism, appeared in his many masterful essays, which were disregarded or attacked by Left and Right alike. Although he had always suffered from weak lungs, Orwell exposed himself during World War II to exhaustion and privation, serving as an air-raid warden when he was rejected by the army. A mortally ill man by the end of the war, he wrote his two masterpieces, *Animal Farm* (1945) and *1984*, before his death on January 23, 1950. Ironically, his only real popular success came after his death.

SYNOPSIS

A prize boar on the Jones Farm, old Major, arrives at just this insight which he explains to his fellow animals. Old Major tells of a life "miserable, laborious, and short". He continues, "We are born, we are given just so much food as will keep the breath in our bodies, and those of us who are capable of it are forced to work to the last atom of our strength; and the very instant that our usefulness has come to an end we are slaughtered with hideous cruelty. No animal in England is free .... Is this simply a part of the order of nature? Is it because this land of ours is so poor that it cannot afford a decent life to those who dwell upon it? No, comrades, a thousand times no!"

Old Major dies, but not before his message takes root. Snowball, Napoleon, and other young pigs preach revolution. The animals are won over. "Animalist" doctrine spreads quickly, and one day, when Mr Jones is forced to leave the farm, the animals establish control.

When Jones and his neighbours try to recapture the farm with firearms, Snowball leads a successful resistance. Initially, the revolution has excellent results. Morale is high. A successful literacy campaign is waged. Pigeons carry the revolutionary message far and wide, while Snowball organises committees to improve the living conditions. The animals labour heroically, especially the powerful Boxer. Just as the future begins to look really bright — Snowball devises a windmill which will reduce the amount of work the animals will have to do — Napoleon springs a *coup d'etat*. Snarling dogs reared from birth by Napoleon chase Snowball away. Though puzzled, Boxer and the other animals develop implicit faith in "our leader, Comrade

Napoleon". "Napoleon is always right," says Boxer. Only the wise old donkey, Benjamin, Boxer's loyal friend, is sceptical.

Methodically, every trace of equality is stripped away as Napoleon and his fellow pigs turn into a ruling caste. Animalist doctrine is transformed: "All animals are equal" becomes "All animals are equal, but some animals are more equal than others". History is rewritten. Boxer, crippled by overwork, is shipped to the glue factory. Dissidents are killed. Memories of the revolution grow dim.

Finally, Napoleon and cohort acquire human characteristics and make peace with the neighbouring farmers. Farmer Pilkington jokes: "If you have your lower animals to contend with, we have our lower classes!" Pig and human now become indistinguishable to the other animals, one as bad as the other.

CHAPTER STUDIES

Chapter One

Old Major plants the idea of Rebellion.

Lenin — father of the Russian Revolution, represented in *Animal Farm* by Major.

Summary

One night while farmer Jones is having a drunken sleep, the animals of Manor Farm hold a meeting. It has been called by Old Major, a pig, because he wants to tell them about a dream he has had.

Before describing the dream, Old Major first of all describes the miserable lives of hard work and exploitation that the animals are subjected to. "Nearly the whole of the produce of our labour is stolen from us by human beings." Animals are not free; man is the only creature that consumes without producing; man puts animals to death. Old Major preaches rebellion, and unity amongst animals. "All animals are comrades," even wild animals. Major lays down some guidelines: "Whatever goes upon two legs, is an enemy. Whatever goes upon four legs, or has wings, is a friend .... Weak or strong, clever or simple, we are all brothers. All animals are equal."

Major finally tells them of his dream, "of the earth as it will be when Man has vanished". It reminded him of a song, "Beasts of England", which he had known as a little pig. This song has a stirring tune, and tells of "the golden future time" when animals will be free, man will be overthrown and peace and prosperity will come to all animals. It exhorts all animals to work hard for this freedom.

All the animals learn the song, and are so enthusiastic in singing it that they wake up Mr Jones, who breaks up the meeting by shooting pellets into the barn wall.

Commentary

Mr Jones is immediately characterised as irresponsible: "too drunk to remember to shut the pop-holes" (small entrance holes for the hens). Although already drunk, he has "a last glass" before bed. His character is already established as self-indulgent and uncaring.

He is contrasted with Old Major, who commands great respect; partly because of his age and status (a prize boar, i.e. one who has gained prizes in competition against other boars); partly because he is the father of 400 pigs; and partly because the pigs are among the most intelligent of animals. But it seems as if he has the affection of the animals also.

The animals are described coming into the meeting, and they are given some individual characteristics. Boxer and Clover are shown to be caring; they step carefully to avoid hurting any other animals. There is a slightly comic touch in the description of Clover's appearance: she "had never quite got her figure back after her fourth foal" (as if she would want to, by exercising as a human would do). Boxer, who is to be an important character, is described more fully, with his strength, steadiness of character and relative simplicity highlighted. The two sides of Benjamin the donkey are also shown: his bitter cynicism, and his devotion to Boxer. The mare Mollie is also featured for her vain attention-seeking behaviour.

Major's speech starts well, seizing their attention by hints of his death to come. Because of his vast experience, he feels qualified to speak on such a serious topic as "the nature of life on this earth". He keeps their attention by focussing on key questions — "What is the nature of this life of ours?" and "But is this simply part of the order of nature?" The answers are drawn out clearly — that their "lives are miserable, laborious and short" — and "remove Man from the scene, and the root cause of hunger and overwork is abolished forever''.

He is a very good speaker, with a command of rhetoric, rhythm, repetition, and practical examples. He appeals to different sections of his audience by referring to them directly — "You cows"; "You hens"; "You, Clover". He refers to the milk, eggs and foals not as economic produce, but in terms of family relationship, implying that Man has murdered these animals. He talks about the animals as if they have human feelings.

Questions on Chapter One

1. Why does Old Major command so much respect?
2. What makes Benjamin so different from the other animals? Is there anything to admire in him?
3. What are (a) the faults of Mollie and the cat, and (b) the virtues of Boxer and Clover?
4. "Man is the only creature that consumes without producing." How does Old Major prove this?
5. What "commandments" does Old Major give to the animals?
6. Why is the song "Beasts of England" such a success?

Glossary

pop-holes: small entrances to the hen-houses
drew: poured
scullery: room next to the kitchen for cleaning dishes
prize: prize-winning (in a show or competition)
Middle: reference to breed
White boar: male pig on a farm that is kept for breeding
ensconced: seated comfortably
tushes: tusks, long sharp protruding side teeth
rafters: large sloping beams that hold up a roof
cud: food that has been swallowed and brought up again to the mouth from the first stomach of certain animals, e.g. cow and sheep, for further chewing
cynical remark: comment from one who sees little or no good in anything
drew: pulled
trap: a light two-wheeled vehicle
mincing: walking in an affected way; taking little short steps
raven: large shiny black bird with a black beak and a deep unmusical voice

comrades: close companions, especially those who share difficult work or troubles; used as a title in Communist countries

confinements: the time during which a female is about to give birth

rations: fixed (usually limited) daily allowance of food

mangel-wurzels: vegetable with a large round root which can be eaten, often grown on farms as cattle food

charge of number 6:   size of lead pellets

pellets: small balls of metal, fired from a gun

Chapter Two

A Successful Rebellion.

Summary

Old Major dies, but the animals, led by the pigs, start to organise themselves for revolution. The leaders are Napoleon, Snowball and Squealer. They build on the teachings of Old Major, devising a system called animalism, which they explain to the other animals at secret meetings. They have difficulty convincing some animals, who are stupid, and are obstructed by Moses, the tame raven, who tells lies, and consoles the animals with talk of Sugarcandy Mountain, a heaven as reward for their hard life on earth. However, Boxer and Clover are faithful supporters of everything the pigs say.

Mr Jones, the farmer, had been neglecting the farm, allowing his men to become lazy. When the animals are left unfed, they break into the store shed, and Jones starts to whip them. Spontaneously, the animals fight back and drive Jones and his men out. The animals celebrate their victory, and destroy the whips, nose-rings, dog-chains, reins, nose-bags. Boxer sacrifices his straw hat, which actually served the purpose of keeping flies out of his ears. They explore the farm house that the humans had lived in, and agree that no animal should live there. The name "Manor Farm" is changed to "Animal Farm", and the pigs announce that the principles of animalism have been reduced to seven commandments, including: "Whatever goes upon two legs is an enemy" (first commandment), and "All animals are equal" (seventh commandment).

The cows are milked, and some animals are hopeful that they will get a share of it, but Napoleon diverts their attention to the importance of getting in the harvest. When they return from harvesting, the milk has disappeared.

Commentary

This chapter shows how the seeds of revolution — Old Major's ideas — are planted in fertile ground. The pigs, as the most intelligent animals, develop and nurture these ideas — seeds — until the time is ripe. The usual cause of a revolution is a long-standing conflict of interests, with the stronger party in control — in this case, the humans. This could go on forever unless opposition is systematically organised, and then a specific incident causes open fighting. Here, the specific incident is the plundering of the store-shed by the animals (who had not been fed) and their spontaneous revolt when they are cruelly whipped.

Napoleon is immediately characterised as the forceful type: "not much of a talker, but with a reputation for getting his own way". His strength is direct, brute force. Snowball, in contrast, talks better and has more ideas, but is less forceful. These are the undoubted leaders, but their chief assistant is Squealer, "a brilliant talker", who can put across the message of animalism very clearly.

All of this is based on the Russian Revolution (1917) with Napoleon representing Stalin, a ruthless dictator, and Snowball a mixture of Lenin and Trotsky, who were more idealistic. "Animalism" represents the ideals of Communism, a political system in which everything is shared equally, and class distinction is abolished. Some do not like change of any kind, and do not realise how they are being used by a ruling class (represented by Mr Jones) and some are just too lazy to do anything about it. ("At the beginning they met with such stupidity and apathy.") The revolutionaries had trouble with the Christian teachings of accepting hardship in this world for reward in the next ("Sugarcandy Mountain"). Moses the tame raven represents organised religion, which is seen as a means of exploiting the masses for the benefit of the small ruling class by making them accept their lot. Karl Marx ("Old Major") claimed that "religion is the opium of the people".

Boxer and Clover represent the unthinking working class, who are so easily led by either good or bad leaders. They are not intelligent enough to examine the details of arguments, and once they have accepted the pigs as leaders, they give them their blind obedience. They are unable to see, or imagine, that their own kind can betray them.

The spontaneous revolt by the animals against Jones and his men (p. 18) shows how a ruling class can go into decline, and that this is the pattern of history. Jones loses interest, starts to drink, neglects to supervise his men, and the whole system falls apart. The Roman Empire, for example, which was built on strict discipline, crumbled into decline when its rulers became more interested in fun, feasting and drinking to excess. The details, however, are very specific to England, and the behaviour is typical of a selfish, lazy type at weekends. The "Red Lion" is a common name for a public house selling beer, and *The News of the World* a lurid newspaper concentrating on sex and violence. The "sudden uprising" when the animals fight back against cruelty, has the advantage of surprise and, like all bullies, Jones and his men are cowards who soon run away; Mrs Jones and Moses also flee, since they belong to the vanquished ruling class.

All the whips and chains (symbolising the repressive machinery of a police state, which keeps down the population by brute force) are destroyed. Even horses' ribbons, as the mark of humans, are destroyed, and Boxer shows a simple-minded sense of sacrifice in burning his straw-hat, which should have been an exception.

The issuing of free rations and the repeated singing of the patriotic song "Beasts of England" reflects the extreme joy felt by a nation that wins a long war. The reality of it all takes some time to sink in, and even the next day they are still surveying the farm that they now control "with speechless admiration". When the animals see inside the farmhouse, it represents the common people seeing inside a palace, seeing the luxurious standards. The agreement that "no animal must ever live there", like Snowball's decree that "all animals should go naked" becomes a broken promise. Mollie represents the class who is selfishly interested only in privileges, like sugar and ribbons. There is a ridiculous touch in the hams being taken out for burial, and the beer being destroyed. The fact that nothing else is touched in the farmhouse shows good discipline, for often a victorious army, or mob uprising, wreck and loot everything they can lay their hands on.

The fact that the pigs can read and write singles them out as the leaders of the animals. In history, the oppressed working classes have often been led by students, political theorists and intellectuals. The right to self-determination is often shown in changing the name of the country, especially if a colonial power has been thrown out.

The pigs have reduced the principles of animalism, which all the animals had understood in general when listening to Old Major, to seven "unalterable" commandments. (The irony, of course, is that all seven are eventually broken.) They were written prominently for all to see from "thirty yards away". All new constitutions are given general, idealistic approval, only to be later revised, and abused to suit the new ruling elite.

The ordinary animals can be manipulated by a call to joint effort and sacrifice in getting in the harvest, and their attention is diverted away from the milk, which is the first sign that the pigs, even at the very start, are corrupt.

Questions on Chapter Two

1. What comic touches do you find in this chapter?
2. What are the faults of Mr Jones, the farmer?
3. Why is it easy for the pigs to establish dominance over the other animals?
4. What is the importance of the song "Beasts of England"?
5. What is Orwell trying to say about "clever" and ordinary people?
6. What differences can you already discern between Snowball and Napoleon?

Glossary

vivacious: lively, outgoing
porker: castrated pig, raised for food
elaborated: worked out in detail
expounded: explained and made clear
apathy: lack of interest
linseed cake: cattle feed
Windsor chair: armchair with high side supports
carpet bag: travel bag originally made of carpet; associated with political exploiters, people who come and go quickly
knoll: small hill
spinney: small wood
lithograph: early type of photograph

Chapter Three

At first, happy co-operation.

Summary

The harvest is more successful than in Jones' time, with every animal working efficiently and happily under the direction of the pigs. Boxer is a model worker, with his motto, "I will work harder". It was a time of perfect co-operation, with a few exceptions like Mollie and the cat. Only Benjamin the donkey expresses doubts.

There is more time for leisure, and on Sundays there is no work at all. Instead, there is a meeting, and ceremonies such as the raising of the flag and the singing of the anthem "Beasts of England". However, the pigs dominate the debates, with Napoleon and Snowball always disagreeing.

The pigs organise a system of education, in which all the animals succeed, to varying degrees, in learning to read and write but more ambitious schemes fail. The dogs are good at reading, but only want to read the seven commandments; Benjamin, although a good reader, refuses to read anything. Boxer is too stupid to learn more than a few letters of the alphabet, despite great efforts; the more stupid animals could not even learn the seven commandments by heart. Snowball therefore reduced them to a single saying: "Four legs good, two legs bad". He explains that birds are included, as their wings are considered as legs, and only man, the enemy of all animals, goes on two legs. This maxim is popular, especially with the sheep.

Napoleon disagrees with Snowball's committees and takes away some new-born puppies for private education. The pigs also claim the privilege of apples and milk, and it is explained that this is necessary because the pigs are "brain-workers''. Squealer explains this, and confuses the issue by suggesting that if the pigs failed in their duty of managing the farm, Jones would come back. The animals are so scared that they agree that the apples and milk ''should be reserved **for the pigs alone''**

Leon Trotsky, the intellectual leader of the Bolsheviks after Lenin's death. Stalin distrusted him, seeing in Trotsky a threat to his own power.

Commentary

This chapter shows how the original ideals and success of the revolution are betrayed; and the idea that all animals are equal is lost. This is seen in two main ways: one, that there is a big difference in intelligence among the animals, and two, that they do not all do the same work, either in amount of effort or in productive value. By the end of the chapter, the pigs have persuaded the other animals to accept their different status and privileges. Notice how Orwell links the chapters. Chapter Two ends with the mystery of the missing milk, which is explained at the end of Chapter Three. Likewise, the young pups, trained secretly by Napoleon, will later emerge, as will the conflict between Napoleon and Snowball.

The success of the harvest reflects how anything new brings out a pioneering spirit of idealistic enthusiasm, bringing out the best in everyone. Yet even at this stage, everything is not perfect; the pigs contribute no physical effort, and their instructions of "gee up, comrade!" are unnecessary and ludicrous.And not every animal makes an equal contribution; some, like Mollie and the cat, being lazy and evasive.

"But everyone worked according to his capacity." This echoes the (Communist) ideal, "From each according to his ability, to each according to his need." At this stage, work is a pleasure, and there are no negative values like stealing, grumbling and quarrelling, which seemed to belong to the bad old days. Benjamin represents the type who distrusts anything new, and has a very realistic view of "human nature", implying that people have some selfish drives which are basic and will re-surface when the initial enthusiasm dies down. His "cryptic" answer means it is short and puzzling — you may be able to work out his meaning, but it is not easy. He seems to imply that he has seen it all before, that it is a temporary fashion, and that he will outlast it. In this "golden age", there are many improvements: more leisure, better education, no punishments, hardships or humiliations. They are hard-working and uncritical, and it is only when a flagrant abuse of the principle of equality is noticed — not sharing the apples — that the animals start to show dissatisfaction. Like all politicians, the pigs have answers — first, pseudo-scientific and second, a scare story which has no direct connection with the main issue. This kind of reasoning is often used by people of superior debating ability but no moral scruples. There are other features which have political significance. The flag is a clear reference to the Russian flag which has a hammer (factory workers) and a sickle (farm workers) united on a red background (for the blood of revolutionary fighting). These two symbols correspond to the hoof and the horn on the animals' green flag. The committees represent the many efforts, of Trotsky in particular, to organise the workers for efficiency and productivity, but they are often hopelessly over-ambitious. The emphasis on education has the dual purpose of making the workers more capable, and also of freeing them from their ignorance which kept them as docile slaves not knowing the true state of affairs. The meetings also reflect how the general population take little part in politics, allowing a few to dominate, and being content with the ceremonial part, like singing the anthem. Another political feature is how the original doctrine, which is quite complex and far-reaching, can be watered down and distorted by being reduced to slogans like "Four legs good, two legs bad". This is far too simplistic and dangerously misleading, but like all slogans, it is easy to remember and pleasurable to repeat. As well as controlling the animals' thoughts in this way, the pigs realise that brainwashing is far easier and more effective on the very young, so the more pragmatic Napoleon concentrates on this section of the public, whilst the more idealistic Snowball tries to cater for all.

Questions on Chapter Three

1. Give *two* reasons why the harvest is so successful.
2. What opinion have you formed of Mollie's character?
3. "Donkeys live a long time. None of you has ever seen a dead donkey." What does Benjamin mean?
4. How does Orwell make fun of the "Animal Committees"?
5. Give *three* instances of animal stupidity.
6. What basic mistake has Boxer made?
7. Which of the animals do you most admire and why?
8. What is the significance of what Muriel does?

Glossary

doled out: distributed in small quantities
resolutions: decisions to do something
paddock: small enclosed field
manipulation: use of the hands
maxim: general rule

Chapter Four

The Battle of the Cowshed.

Summary

News about Animal Farm has spread over the country, and Napoleon and Snowball are promoting revolution on other farms. Jones does not get much sympathy from the other farmers, and the immediate neighbours of Animal Farm, Mr Pilkington and Mr Frederick, dislike each other intensely. They both worry about their own animals rebelling, and start rumours to discredit Animal Farm, but the song "Beasts of England" becomes very popular throughout the country, as the mood of rebellion spreads amongst animals, making the humans fearful.

Jones attempts to retake Animal Farm by force, but he is outwitted by Snowball, who tricks them into thinking they have won, but leads Jones' gang into an ambush, where they are surrounded, and then chased away by the animals. Boxer is very sad because he thinks he has killed a stable-boy, but in fact, the boy is only stunned, and recovers. The animals celebrate and bury the sheep that has been killed. Snowball emphasises the need for all animals to be ready to die for Animal Farm if need be.

Boxer, Snowball and the dead sheep are awarded a medal each for their bravery. The battle is called The Battle of the Cowshed, and this day and the anniversary of the Rebellion are to be commemorated each year, by the firing of the gun captured from Jones.

Commentary

Again, the events follow closely the events of the Russian Revolution. News spreads to other countries, and the

leaders, Snowball and Napolean, recognise that it is important to spread the ideas of revolution outside of their own
territory.

Many of the Russian ruling class went into exile in places
like Paris, and this is represented comically as Jones sitting
in the pub complaining (like Imelda Marcos in Hawaii).

The first reaction to the Russian Revolution was fear that
it would spread world-wide. Consequently, hostile governments suppressed too much publicity, and cast scorn on the
idea of workers being able to manage a country. They still
referred to "Russia" rather than the new name ("U.S.S.R."),
and spread various unfounded rumours about it.

However, these rumours were replaced by news of
success, and this encourages other countries to experience
the beginnings of revolution and self-assertion by the
oppressed classes.

Every revolution is followed by a counter-revolution (e.g.
in Nicaragua, where the opposition to the revolutionary
government are called "Contras" — "against") and this is
represented in a somewhat comical fashion by the attempt
by Jones to recapture the farm. The battle is described in
military terms such as "skirmish", "manoeuvre" and
"second line of attack", but the weaponry is ridiculous, such
as the pigeons "bombing" Jones with their droppings. It
is also comically ludicrous to compare a barn-yard fight to
the campaigns of Julius Caesar, yet it makes the point that
revolutions are often led by intellectuals (like Snowball) who
adapt their reading to practical military use.

The battle itself is described with a lot of movement,
building to a climax — "they were gored, kicked, bitten,
trampled on." The heroes are Snowball and Boxer, and even
the cat, normally so evasive, takes part, to show how all
sections of society will combine against a common enemy.

The seriousness is always balanced by something light and humorous, such as Jones being hurled into a pile of dung. The nobility of Boxer is illustrated by his sorrow at taking life, and the ruthlessness needed for a revolution to succeed is shown by Snowball's advice to Boxer to avoid feelings of sympathy for an enemy — "War is war. The only good human being is a dead one."

The self-centredness of each animal is indicated by the phrase "each recounting his own exploits", and the celebrations enhance the feelings of patriotism, as the animals develop their own traditions; recognising and decorating heroes, and establishing commemorative ceremonies, as every new nation must do.

Questions on Chapter Four

1. How important is it to know about the events of the Russian Revolution, even in outline? Why?
2. Is it human nature to want to turn someone else's misfortune to your own advantage? What example do we see of this in Chapter Four?
3. Why do you think that the rumours about Animal Farm "were never fully believed"?
4. Why is the song "Beasts of England" so important, and so successful?
5. Comment on the contributions made by the various animals (including Napoleon) to the victory.
6. How does Orwell achieve a balance between the serious and the comic? Why does he include the comic elements?

Glossary

tap room: room reserved for males in a pub
Willingdon: neighbouring village

had their females in common: shared their wives; were
                                                      promiscuous
tractable: obedient
muted: defecated; released droppings
fifteen stone: about a hundred kilos (a stone is a little over
                             six kilos)
gored: pierced with a horn
ignominious: shameful
impromptu: spontaneous; unplanned

Chapter Five

Napoleon drives out Snowball and seizes total power.

Summary

Mollie runs away, and is seen pulling a cart for a publican, happy that she is being spoilt and getting a lot of attention.

The animals hold many meetings, but there are always disputes between Snowball, a brilliant talker and full of new ideas, and Napoleon, who ensures that he has strong support by talking personally to the animals, especially the sheep, who are encouraged to interrupt Snowball's convincing speeches by bleating the slogan "Four legs good, two legs bad."

Snowball proposes the building of a windmill, to provide electrical power which would lead to a three-day working week. Napoleon argues against this idea, saying that they need to spend all their effort on food production, or starve. The animals divide into two groups under the slogans "Vote for Snowball and the three-day week" and "Vote for Napoleon and the full manger". Only Benjamin refuses to join either group, disbelieving the promises made by the leaders.

Another dispute was about the defence of the farm, in the event of an attack by Jones. Snowball proposed stirring up rebellion on other farms, whilst Napoleon suggested obtaining and using firearms. The animals could not decide which one to support.

At a meeting to take a vote on whether to build the windmill proposed by Snowball, Napoleon says little, and the animals are won over by Snowball's vision of a wonderful future. Before a vote could be taken, however, Napoleon sets nine dogs on Snowball, who is chased out of the farm.

These were the puppies raised and trained in private by Napoleon to secure his power.

Lenin addresses a meeting in Moscow. The figure in uniform on the right is Trotsky, who played a vital role in the October revolution but was removed from power after Lenin's death, sent into exile and finally assassinated. Sometimes this photograph is used with the figure of Trotsky eliminated, just as Snowball was 'eliminated' by Napoleon.

Napoleon announces that the Sunday morning meetings would end, with no more debates. All decisions would be taken by the pigs, presided over by Napoleon. The animals do not like this, but they are menaced into silence by the dogs, and the continuous bleating of "Four legs good, two legs bad!" prevents any discussion.

Squealer is sent round the farm to explain the new order. He claims that Napoleon is sacrificing himself in order to lead, and that Snowball was a criminal, suggesting that he did not really fight bravely in the Battle of the Cowshed. The animals, threatened with the return of Jones, accept the argument, and Boxer adopts the motto "Napoleon is always right".

The animals still meet on Sunday mornings, but now they are divided into two groups. The pigs and the dogs are on a raised platform facing the rest of the animals. Now, Napoleon reads out the orders of the week, and the only participation by the rest is to sing "Beasts of England".

Later, Napoleon surprises everyone by saying that the windmill will be built after all. Squealer is sent to tell the animals that it was in fact Napoleon's original idea, stolen by Snowball. When asked why Napoleon had so strongly opposed it, Squealer claimed that Napoleon had only *seemed* to oppose it, as a tactic to get rid of Snowball. Despite this illogical argument, Squealer is persuasive and since the dogs are also so threatening, the animals accept his explanation.

Commentary

Mollie represents selfishness and vanity. She is unable to discipline herself to hard work for the sake of the common good. Her defection is caused by the temptations of sugar and ribbons, luxuries unobtainable on Animal Farm. In any revolution, certain classes, used to privileges, are unwilling to make sacrifices, to join with the poor and downtrodden in a common striving to improve the lot of everyone. Her new owner is described unfavourably — overweight, unhealthy- looking, and with poor taste in clothes. The pigeons who bring the information represent spies, or intelligence agents.

The cold weather means less time for work, more for meetings. Already the leadership of the pigs is unquestioned, although their decisions on planning and farm policy had to be approved by a majority vote of all the animals. Although this is usually a formality, it is still an important principle — the right to be consulted — with the other animals.

The meetings reveal the political rivalry between able leaders, and the passivity of the majority. Snowball is good on detailed plans, which he has researched, and putting them across to the animals in brilliant public speeches. Napoleon has nothing concrete to offer, but he makes sure of support by "canvassing" — this means organising animals to vote for him, regardless of the arguments put forward in public debate. So, however brilliant Snowball is, the sheep, for instance, will always vote for Napoleon. Another tactic is to manipulate the meetings by interruptions, so that Snowball's main points ("at the crucial moments") are obscured. To keep the atmosphere of a fairy story, because the political message is a bit heavy, Orwell introduces a comical effect by the mock gravity of "a complicated scheme for all the animals to drop their dung directly in the fields, at a different spot every day, to save the labour of cartage".

Snowball's plan for the windmill represents the industrialisation needed to make an agricultural nation a modern one. (Russia before the 1917 revolution had been a feudal state with the ordinary people little more than slaves). Snowball is an intellectual (gently mocked by the titles of the down-to-earth books that he reads) and a visionary. Napoleon is more interested in power for power's sake, and will use any means to achieve it, with brute force (the dogs), indoctrination (of the sheep) or unfair tactics (using the sheep to interrupt Snowball's speeches). Whereas Snowball appeals to idealism, Napoleon concentrates on the baser instincts — greed and self-preservation, in this case "the full manger". His response to Snowball's eloquence, and detailed, ingenious planning, is typically primitive — he "urinated over the plans, and walked out without uttering a word". He cannot use words, except in the form of simplistic slogans — "Four legs good, two legs better" and "Vote for Napoleon and the full manger".

Benjamin is a cynic and is not attracted by any promises, having a gloomy view of life, or perhaps of the motives of those who control our lives.

The question of the defence of the farm is also a contentious issue — the animals are divided between the long-term view and the short-term view. Snowball's solution is to spread so much revolution that Animal Farm will not be the only outpost of revolution, and thus will attract less attention. Also, of course, the other revolutions will (a) take up all the efforts of the opposition (man) and (b) make the new order acceptable. Napoleon's viewpoint is immediate survival. This need is there, it is true, but it will always be there if one allows a "siege mentality" to develop. Snowball is all for developing, or improving the situation through foresight, while Napoleon limits himself to immediate needs. The animals are portrayed as being easily led, changing opinion readily.

The climax is built up carefully by the two contrasted speeches of Snowball and Napoleon. Napoleon offers no competition to Snowball, but the sheep do, and it is Snowball's intelligence and eloquence against the sheep's stupidity and inability to express themselves which motivates Snowball into an impassioned and imaginative vision of progress. Just when Snowball is about to triumph, Napoleon pulls his master-stroke — the release of the savage dogs on Snowball.

The quiet that follows the expulsion of Snowball reflects the shock of the animals, and they are further disappointed to notice how the dogs wagged their tails at Napoleon just as the other dogs had to Jones. All the old evils are returning, and more are to come as freedom of speech and decision-making is taken away from the majority. The animals are not able to express their disquiet, and the young pigs who try are frightened into silence by the dogs (the secret police). The sheep represent the stupid majority who accept all the government propaganda, and talk in cliches.

Squealer's job is public relations — to make Napoleon's actions seem good, and make Snowball a scapegoat for all problems. He deals in downright lies — "No one believes more firmly than Comrade Napoleon that all animals are equal" — which are obscured by exaggerated claims, for instance, that Snowball is "a criminal". His two other tricks are revisionism — to "revise" history (such as Snowball's undoubted courage) and to exploit fear, "Surely, comrades, you don't want Jones back?". Unfortunately, the animals do not have the intelligence to see through this smoke-screen of assertions and lies, and can only simplify it into "Napoleon is always right". This basic assumption is wrong, of course, but the majority usually assume that a government is always right and incorruptible.

The meetings are now a farce, with no participation. It is ironic that instead of decision-making, the animals' attention is diverted by parading past the Skull of Old Major, whose ideals are being broken. (This is suggestive of the masses filing past the tomb of Lenin in Red Square, Moscow.) Minimus represents the need for propaganda, to be able to brainwash a gullible public with songs and slogans, masking their loss of freedom.

The announcement of the amazing change of policy regarding the windmill is typical of information dispersed by tyrants. No reasons are given, and hard work and reduced rations make the news even more confusing, especially as it is announced that the change in policy had been planned in detail.

Squealer's role in "selling" the news is to reverse the truth — to present lies so convincingly that they are believed. The bigger the lie, the more it is believed. The animals are confused by the use of the expression "tactics" to explain Napoleon's role in the windmill debate, and they are also intimidated into silence by the dogs. And since they have no other leader, they must accept that "Napoleon is always right".

Questions on Chapter Five

1. How does Clover try to deal with Mollie?
2. Are Snowball's schemes practical? Give reasons for and against them.
3. How does Snowball sway the animals to vote for the windmill?

4. "Napoleon, with the dogs following him, now mounted on to the raised portion of the floor where Major had previously stood to deliver his speech." What is significant about this?
5. Give two reasons why the animals do not protest about the expulsion of Snowball.
6. How does Napoleon communicate?

Glossary

breeches: short trousers fastened at or below the knee
gaiters: pair of cloth or leather coverings to cover the leg from knee to ankle
publican: one who owns and runs a pub (public house)
ratified: approved
acreage: area of a piece of land measured in acres
canvassing: asking; getting
back numbers: earlier issues
Farmer and Stock Breeder: magazines
silage: fodder stored in a silo away from air for preservation as winter food for cattle
basic slag: lighter glasslike waste material left when metal is separated from its natural rock
cartage: having to be carried (originally by cart) from one place to another
dynamo: machine which turns some other kind of power (in this case, wind) into electricity
cranks: rods
cog-wheels: wheels with teeth (cogs) round the edge
snuffed: sniffed
quarried: dug out
procured: obtained
restive: restless

sordid: very unpleasant
baying: repeated deep cry of large hunting dogs
spurt: short sudden increase of speed
mounted on: got on
marshal: arrange
articulate: able to express themselves clearly
moonshine: unrealistic talk
watchword: word or phrase expressing briefly the principles of a party
disinterred: dug up
stump: base of a tree left after the rest has been cut down
reverent: respectful
advocated: supported

Chapter Six

The windmill is destroyed.

Summary

Work becomes tougher, with work on Sunday afternoons as well. The harvest is less successful, and there is a likelihood of a food shortage. They solve the problem of breaking up the stones by dropping them over the edge of the quarry. Everyone contributes to the effort, with Boxer as an inspiration and example to all. The animals are surviving well without humans around, but because they are short of necessary materials unobtainable on Animal Farm, Napoleon announces a new policy: they will trade with neighbouring farms, and the hens are asked to sacrifice their eggs for this purpose.

The animals are uneasy at these changes, as they had originally passed resolutions never to deal with humans, use money or engage in trade. As usual, any discussion is stopped by the growling of the dogs and the bleating of the sheep. Napoleon will deal with everything personally through Mr Whymper. Again, as usual, Squealer is sent to persuade the animals that no such resolutions were ever passed, as none exist in writing.

Animal Farm gains a new respect from the humans, who now start to use its new name, Manor Farm, and the animals are proud to see Napoleon, on all fours, giving orders to Whymper, on two legs. Jones has given up hope of getting his farm back, and gone away. There is no other contact with the outside world, although there are rumours that Napoleon is negotiating with Pilkington or Frederick.

The pigs move into the farm house and sleep in the beds, and when the animals check whether this breaks the fourth commandment, they see that it now reads "No animal shall sleep in a bed *with sheets*". Squealer explains it all away, and brings up the usual scare story of Jones coming back, so that the animals shut up, even when it is announced that the pigs will get up one hour later.

The hardness of life is compensated for by the progress of the windmill, which delights the animals, except for Benjamin. However, the windmill is blown down in a violent storm and Napoleon puts all the blame on Snowball.

Commentary

The windmill is seen as the "Sugarcandy Mountain", the promised land that is a future reward for present hardships. This is typical of the empty promises of politicians who exploit the willingness of the masses to suffer hardship. Notice how cynically the animals are expected to work on Sundays — it is supposed to be "strictly voluntary" but if they do not work, their rations are cut by half. However, the work on the windmill itself shows the animals at their best, with everyone — even the pigs "at critical moments" — working together. Boxer works the hardest, and makes the most sacrifices of time and effort, inspiring himself with his two mottoes — "I will work harder" and "Napoleon is always right" — and inspiring the other animals by his example. He represents the admirable attitude of ordinary people who unfortunately are not intelligent enough to realise that the basic belief — "Napoleon is always right" is, in fact, untrue.

At this stage, comparing their position to that in Jones's day, the animals are just as well fed, because they do not have "to support five extravagant human beings as well". Although there are failures, the animals are more efficient and honest.

The sudden change in policy is typical of Napoleon. There is no preparation, no discussion, about engaging in trade. The excuse is given that the needs of the windmill must override everything else. One section of the community, as often happens, is hit unfairly, as the hens have to make a personal sacrifice. This is a comment on how centralised government planning ignores individual needs.

The changing of the original ideals of the revolution, the "revising" of these basic ideals (e.g. not to deal with humans) is called revisionism. It was common in Stalin's day for history to be re-written, e.g. all mention of Trotsky, and his photographs, were removed from newspapers, books and accounts of the time. How is this enforced? How is it accepted? First, by intimidation — a formidable secret police (the dogs); second, by a stupid, gullible public (the sheep); third, by propaganda — control of the media, and control of minds. Squealer points out that nothing is written down, so the animals cannot argue from evidence, and the only thing that is written down — the commandments — are re-written without challenge. The animals, without effective leadership (Snowball is in exile, the young porkers are too timid, Benjamin knows but is too passive), are easily convinced by Squealer's persuasiveness. Abuse of privilege by the ruling class is often obscured by the threat of some great calamity — e.g. the return of Jones.

The humans are featured in this chapter. Firstly, they are depicted as parasites — "Five extravagant human beings" — as represented by Jones, his wife and men. The animals can manage more efficiently without them. "Since no animal now stole" implies that stealing was normal in Jones's time, because of the injustice enforced on the animals — they were not getting a fair share of what they produced. Also, there is a contrast in the idealism of the arable land not needing to be fenced, and the co-operative zeal the animals put into an enterprise that will benefit them — the windmill.

The second reference to humans is in the outside world's reaction to Animal Farm. Although hostile, and willing it to failure (e.g. they think that the windmill will never work) they start to accept it, grudgingly, as they recognise that it is efficient. One symptom is the use of the new name. Many people are reluctant to accept change, and the names "U.S.S.R." and "Zimbabwe" sound very unfamiliar to people used to "Russia" and "Rhodesia". (Names like "Zhenghua" for Bukit Panjang are unrecognisable to some people, especially the older generation). The acceptance is complete in the sense that they do not expect Jones to regain the farm (he has gone away, defeated) and that they have started trade with the humans on equal terms. The significant development, however, is the changed relationship between animal and man. Napoleon is giving *orders* to Whymper. He is presented in a poor light — a money-grabbing opportunist of no principles whatsoever. The final reference to humans is to powerful men, Pilkington and Frederick, both farm owners, and the rumours about their negotiations with Napoleon foreshadow their future involvement. Napoleon is smart enough to keep them both guessing, however, to show that he is not at an intellectual disadvantage.

To show how any revolution can become corrupted by a ruling elite, we see the pigs abusing power by adopting the lifestyle of the former rulers. The irony is that the revolution was to overthrow such unfair class distinctions and privileges, but now the palaces (the farmhouse, which was supposed to become a museum), the titles ("the leader"), and the comforts (the beds) are for the pigs alone. They have already taken the apples and milk (which even

Snowball agreed to, so he was not completely democratic), done away with democratic meetings, sleep one hour longer, have special guards (the dogs), deal with humans and now they are breaking the fourth commandment — sleeping in beds. Their answer, through Squealer, is a rationalisation to baffle the animals — there is nothing wrong with a *bed*, just a bed with sheets. While they are trying to think that out, the issue is hidden under the smoke-screen of Jones coming back.

Despite the hardships, and these changes in ideals, the animals are "tired but happy" as "the windmill compensated for everything". They see the windmill as the fulfilment of a dream, something that will be worth all the effort, a supreme motivation. It is the materialistic answer to the religious "Sugarcandy Mountain".

It should be obvious to everyone that the ruin of the windmill is the result of a natural disaster, but Napoleon is able to put the blame on Snowball. The sad thing is that the animals accept this smear as truth, and henceforward Napoleon can use Snowball as a scapegoat for any misfortune. The death sentence is pronounced without any formal trial, or evidence, or defence allowed.

All normal rights are disappearing. The animals are convinced even before Napoleon gives his flimsy "evidence". He himself "pronounced" the footprints to be Snowball's, and it was his "opinion" that Snowball had "probably" come from Foxwood Farm. All this has no factual foundation, but simple minds can be convinced by a rousing speaker, who ends with an emotional, patriotic climax.

Questions on Chapter Six

1. What is the attitude of the animals to work, harsh conditions and setbacks?

2. In what *two* ways does Boxer excel?
3. How are the humans presented in this chapter?
4. How do the pigs manage to prevent any dissent from the animals?
5. Do you find any touches of humour in this chapter?
6. What methods does Squealer use to manipulate the animals?

Glossary

yoked: put in wooden bar used for joining the two animals together in order to pull heavy loads

matted: hair tangled in a mass

pasture: land where grass, used as food for cattle, is grown

arable: land used for growing crops

override: make more important than anything else

resolutions: decisions

solicitor: lawyer

broker: person who does the business of buying and selling for another

commissions: amount of money, usually related to the value of goods bought and sold, paid to the broker for his services

reconciled them: caused them to accept

dropped their championship: gave up their support

drawing room: living room

repose: rest

reassured: confirmed in opinion; again made (Squealer) feel sure

compensated: made up

perpendicularity: quality of being exactly upright

imposing: powerful in appearance; strong; large in size

elm tree ... plucked up like a radish: the tree was completely uprooted, plucked up like a vegetable, to
   indicate how strong the winds were
with one accord: with everybody agreeing
malignity: desire to cause evil
ignominious: shameful
indignation: anger over injustice or wickedness

Chapter Seven

Things get Worse.

Summary

Cold, and usually hungry, the animals slave to rebuild the windmill, and only Boxer and Clover never lose heart. The humans think the windmill collapsed through faulty design, although the animals still believe it was destroyed by Snowball.

The animals face starvation but, determined to keep the news from the outside world, Napoleon uses Whymper to spread the impression that food supplies are good. Napoleon, now rarely seen, announces that eggs will be sold to pay for food stuffs. The hens rebel, but are ruthlessly defeated by the dogs. This news is kept from Whymper.

Napoleon negotiates alternately with Frederick and Pilkington about the sale of some timber. Snowball becomes the scapegoat for everything that goes wrong on the farm. Squealer reveals that he is plotting with Frederick to capture the farm, and that he was secretly in league with Jones from the very start. He even claims that Snowball tried to get the animals defeated at the Battle of the Cowshed. Even the trusting Boxer does not believe this, since Snowball was awarded a medal for bravery. Squealer claims that Napoleon was the real hero, and Boxer is only convinced when Squealer insists that Napoleon said that Snowball was, in fact, a traitor from the very beginning ("If Comrade Napoleon says it, it must be right"). However, Squealer does not like Boxer's objections.

At a special assembly, four pigs are dragged forward by the dogs to Napoleon's feet. Three dogs try to attack Boxer, but he is too strong for them. The four pigs then confess to plotting with Snowball about the windmill, and the seiz-ing of the farm by Frederick. They are then killed by the dogs. Other animals make ridiculous confessions and are executed immediately.

The animals are bewildered by these killings for "since Jones left the farm, until today, no animal had killed another animal". Boxer decides it must be due to some fault in themselves, and the solution is to work harder. Clover looks out over the beautiful scenery of the farm, and remembers the picture of freedom, equality, mutual protection and help inspired by Major's speeches. Although confused, and repelled by the violence, she is still loyal to Napoleon. Unable to express her feelings, she leads the animals in a mournful singing of "Beasts of England".

Squealer announces Napoleon's decree that "Beasts of England" has been abolished, and it was forbidden to sing it. He explains that now that the rebellion is complete, with all external and internal enemies defeated, it has no more purpose. It expressed the "longing for a better society" but since that had already been established, the song was no longer needed. Any objection is prevented by the usual bleating of the sheep. In place of the song is a new one by Minimus the poet, but the animals do not like either its words or tune.

Commentary

The humans know the windmill was destroyed because it was poorly designed, but the animals still believe Napoleon's explanation that it was destroyed by Snowball. Public relations, how the farm appears to "the outside world" (human and animal), is important, so news of food shortages is first concealed and then falsified. Since the humans already had heard wild rumours, Napoleon made sure that Whymper was given a specially good impression of the food situation. "A few selected animals, mostly sheep", are part of this deception.

Napoleon becomes increasingly remote and authoritarian, seldom appearing in public. He uses "remote control", issuing his orders through Squealer, and protecting himself, and keeping away from casual contact, by the fierce dogs. This shows either contempt for the ordinary animals — he does not bother to speak to them, mix with them, let alone consult them — or fear that they may assassinate him.

The rebellion by the hens is because Napoleon has gone too far, and they cannot accept his proposal to sell their eggs. It is a matter of principle for them, but their resistance is soon crushed, and covered up, so that the outside world does not hear of any dissatisfaction. This distortion of news is essential to any tyrannical rule, and the facts — starvation, executions, internal rebellion — are kept secret.

There is now a sustained campaign to discredit Snowball, and to "re-write history" to make a hero into a villain. He becomes the scapegoat for everything that goes wrong, even when it can be disproved (as with the key), or even when the accusation is comically ridiculous (the cows claim that Snowball milked them in their sleep). The only "evidence" is provided by Napoleon, who claims that he can scent Snowball all over the farm.

The next stage in the discrediting of Snowball is to invent the fact that he was Jones' secret agent from the very beginning. The evidence, of course, is very flimsy — probably forged "documents" which the poor animals are not clever enough to read, and, very strangely, these documents have only recently been discovered. From the animals' point of view, of course, this could be true — they already believe that Snowball destroyed the windmill, and they are in no position to challenge the "documents" — but they are then asked to disbelieve the evidence of their own eyes, namely, that Snowball did *not* fight bravely at the Battle of the Cowshed. Even the loyal, stupid Boxer cannot swallow this, and the lie is made even bigger by Squealer's false claim that Napoleon was the real hero. (He took no part in the battle.) Boxer cannot be convinced about Snowball until Squealer says that Napoleon says so. Squealer's statement reveals the importance of this confrontation between the official version and the truth. He speaks "slowly" and "firmly" and repeats the word "categorically" twice, for absolute emphasis. The "ugly look" he casts at Boxer obviously hints that Boxer, despite his exemplary work-ethic and absolute loyalty, is not safe from Napoleon's reign of terror. The attack (by the dogs) on Boxer was obviously aimed at killing him, and the reason was probably that, despite his stupidity, he was capable of leadership because of his example. What he says would be respected by the other animals, and Napoleon was intent on eliminating all *potential* opposition, even those, like Boxer, who are useful and loyal.

Becoming more and more the typical despot, Napoleon awards himself medals — a meaningless act, since awards should be recognition from someone else. Of course, the only opinion that Napoleon values is his own. The atmosphere of terror is now complete, and the dogs make everyone frightened. Napoleon tries to eliminate opposition and intimidate the rest by forced public "confessions" and executions. Boxer is so unsuspecting and loyal that he does not kill the dog, even though he could — he just waits for Napoleon's decision, probably not realising that his own life is threatened. The public spectacle of it all will have a dramatic effect on the animals — throats are torn out in a brutal manner, and Napoleon speaks in a "terrible" voice. As well as terrifying the animals (some of the "confessions"

are of trivial or even imaginary "crimes") the trials serve
the additional purpose of implicating Snowball in all the
crimes. There is a sense of excess, of "overkill", in the pile
of corpses, and the air "heavy with the smell of blood".

It is difficult for the animals to recover from such a shocking spectacle but the sad thing is that they do not question
the "treachery" of the animals said to be in league with
Snowball, or the suitability of the death sentence for some
trivial, as well as serious offences. They have reached an
important moral boundary — no animal has killed another
animal. It is implied that maybe the rats are so untrust-
worthy that maybe they deserve to be killed, but even they
have survived. Significantly, the cat, with a fine sense of
self-preservation, had suddenly disappeared before the
assembly. Boxer is so stupid, so self-critical that he assumes
that they, and not Napoleon, are at fault. He is unable to
reason that he has witnessed a terrible injustice, and is made
to believe that if such terrible vengeance has been exacted,
it *must* have been deserved. His solution of more self-
sacrifice, is sad, because such unanalytical nobility is always
exploited by the likes of Napoleon. Boxer does not even
realise that Napoleon intended to kill him!

Whilst Boxer is much admired by the other animals,
Clover provides them with emotional comfort. She is the
mother figure to them all, protective and caring.

Questions on Chapter Seven

1. How do the humans get their information about Animal
   Farm?
2. Squealer talks about "The joy of service and the dignity
   of labour". What is ironic about this?
3. Name *three* different types of rumour in this chapter.
4. How is Snowball discredited?

5. What different types of opposition to Napoleon are there, and how are they dealt with?
6. How does Napoleon control information and "truth"?
7. What is the climax of this chapter?

Glossary

infanticide: killing their young
clutches: a set of eggs laid by a hen
pullets: young hens during their first year of laying eggs
thwart: successfully oppose
decreed: officially ordered
capitulated: surrendered
coccidiosis: hen disease (fatal)
attribute it to: believe it to be the result of
in league with: working secretly together with
stupefied: so surprised they were unable to think
graphically: clearly; in a lifelike manner
categorically: unconditionally
lurking: hiding
cowered: bent low and drew back in fear
countenance: the expression on his face
whereat: at which
slunk away: frightened; moved quietly away
tumult: confusion
collaborated: worked together
incited: encouraged; stirred up
secreted: concealed
retribution: deserved punishment
gilded: brightened as if with gold

Chapter Eight

Napoleon becomes power mad.

Summary

The animals, uneasy at the killings, are reassured to read that the sixth commandment says: "No animal shall kill any other animal *without cause*". They accept that traitors plotting with Snowball deserve death.

Work seems harder than in Jones' day but Squealer disproves this with statistics. However, the animals "would sooner have less figures and more food".

A personality cult arises around Napoleon, with more privileges for himself, fewer public appearances, and "every successful achievement and stroke of good fortune" credited to him. He has a new title, the gun is fired on his birthday, and the animals accept it all. The two agents of this image-making are Minimus and Squealer.

Rumours about dealings with Pilkington, Frederick and Snowball abound. Three hens confess to plotting to kill Napoleon, inspired by Snowball, and are executed. Napoleon has arranged to sell the timber to Pilkington, and friendly relations are established. Frederick, however, is seen as a cruel monster to his own animals, and as one determined to destroy the nearly completed windmill. Napoleon denies that he has ever had dealings with Frederick and changes the slogan "Death to Humanity" to "Death to Frederick". Snowball is blamed for the weeds in the wheat crop, and it was explained that he had never been decorated for bravery, but in fact had been blamed for cowardice. This bewilders the animals, but Squealer soon persuades them that their memories are at fault.

Stalin, who is represented by Napoleon in *Animal Farm*.

The windmill, newly completed, is called Napoleon Windmill. Napoleon amazes the animals by announcing that he has sold the timber to Frederick. The slogan "Death to Frederick" is changed to "Death to Pilkington". Squealer explains that because Napoleon cunningly seemed to be friendly with Pilkington, Frederick was forced to pay a high price — and in cash, not by cheque. However, the bank-notes are forgeries, and the death sentence is pronounced on Frederick.

Frederick and his men attack the farm, and blow up the windmill. The animals, enraged, return to the attack and win a fierce battle. Despite the death of many animals and the destruction of the windmill, Squealer claims it is a victory to be celebrated, even though Boxer knows that they are in a worse position than before. However, the celebrations are a great morale booster, and conveniently cover up the humiliation of the bank-note confidence trick.

The pigs get drunk on whisky, and Squealer announces that Napoleon is dying, poisoned by Snowball's agents. Napoleon's last decree on earth is that drinking alcohol was to be punishable by death. However, he recovers, buys some books on brewing and distilling, and plants some barley (necessary for brewing). The fifth commandment is now seen to read: "No animal shall drink alcohol *to excess*."

Commentary

The animals are too stupid to remember the original commandments and are easily manipulated into believing the revised versions. Their instincts of what is right (e.g. that no animal shall kill another under any circumstances) are corrupted by unquestioning acceptance of two unproven facts — one, that Snowball is a traitor, and two, that the executed animals were plotting with him. This shows how a ruling elite can engineer a gullible public into believing anything by controlling information, distorting the truth and eliminating intelligent opposition.

Another example is economic. The animals instinctively know they are working harder and eating less, but statistics paint a glowing picture. Because they have no clear memory or hard evidence of pre-revolution days, the animals are reluctantly convinced.

The basis of the original revolution, that all animals are equal, and that humans are the enemy, is now ruthlessly ignored as Napoleon grabs even more power, in order to make himself way above the animals, like a demi-god. The cult of personality means brainwashing the masses into believing that one man (Stalin in Russia, Mao Ze Dong in China, Big Brother in Orwell's *1984*) is responsible for every success. This is done by plastering his picture and his sayings everywhere, yet keeping him remote from close scrutiny. Far from the revolution being organised by a committee of equals, all power and credit is given to one man, so that the masses can identify with a father-figure hero. Even among the pigs, Napoleon now lives and eats alone, claiming other self-important privileges. His titles are quite humorous, and some of the claims quite ridiculous, such as giving Napoleon the credit for the taste of the water.

National anthems or poems should be solemn, dignified, and inspiring. The poem about Napoleon is laughable, embarrassing doggerel. (Doggerel is unpoetical verse, poor in rhythm, rhyme, meaning and expression.) Napoleon is far from a "Friend of the fatherless", the animals do not have a "Full belly twice a day", nor do they sleep "at peace". The expression "Lord of the swill-bucket" is far from dignified, and the idea of a young pig "squeaking" out Napoleon's name is also ludicrously undignified. There are some attempts at poetic language, such as the archaic "thee", "thy", "thou" and "ere", but the overall effect is satirical.

The fact that it is put up near to the Seven Commandments, thereby equating personal praise with fundamental ideals, shows how important Napoleon now thinks himself to be, and how debased the values have become. Of course, all of this is decided by Napoleon himself, from the celebration of his birthday as a "national" event to the awarding of medals to himself. The insincerity of Squealer in putting all this across is masked by his good acting ability, as he can make tears roll down his cheeks.

The negotiations with the humans, Frederick and Pilkington, represent "the cold war" in the sense that every nation cannot exist in total isolation (as seen in the recent example of Burma) but must deal with enemies for economic or political advantage. Napoleon's negotiations are completely without moral scruple, as he changes his tactics and allegiances for no good reason. His stated intention is to play off the two against each other, to get the best price. Regardless of Frederick's threats to destroy the windmill and his reputed cruelty to animals, Napoleon still deals with him because that is how he eventually gets the best price for the timber. He tells lies about this, even though he publicly denounces Frederick. (This can be compared to modern countries who denounce *apartheid* yet secretly trade with South Africa.) The flow of information, however, is always controlled by Napoleon, so that he can, for example, slander Snowball, and blame him for everything going wrong, as well as "revise" his part in history. Notice that rebellion is not promoted on Foxwood, Mr Pilkington's farm, as Napoleon is becoming friendly with Mr Pilkington. The animals are kept in control by rumours of attack by Frederick, and are completely deceived by Napoleon's secret treaty with him. Squealer praises Napoleon's skilful diplomacy, but in fact, Napoleon is out-manoeuvred and cheated by Frederick. This goes to show that there can be no trust or honest dealings between those who have no moral decency. Of course, a former "friend", now betrayed, will not help, and Pilkington takes pleasure in telling Napoleon, "Serves you right". (This episode recalls the non-aggression pact signed by Germany and Russia in 1939, only for Germany to invade Russia in 1940.)

In the battle, Boxer is again prominent, and surprisingly, Napoleon makes efforts to rally the animals. He directs operations "from the rear" (in safety) but his strategy is effective. He gets a comically trivial wound (the tip of his tail is chipped) compared to the deaths and serious injuries inflicted on the others. The importance of propaganda, that is, of promoting a favourable but distorted view of events, is shown in how the animals are convinced they have won a victory. The facts are that the windmill is destroyed and they have several dead, but this is glossed over as the animals are distracted by rewards, songs, speeches and celebrations. It is a classic way to present news in wartime, in order to keep up morale. It also disguises the fact that Napoleon misjudged Frederick's character and intentions in the first place.

The episode of the pigs drinking alcohol is quite comic in presentation, but shows how a ruling class always becomes corrupt, and cannot resist pleasure and privilege. The hypocrisy of it all is quite obvious and amusing, as Napoleon is certainly not dying, but feeling sorry for himself as he is suffering from a self-inflicted hangover (the depressing after-effects of excess alcohol "hang over" all day afterwards). He wants sympathy and attention, and turns something he should be ashamed of into a national crisis. However, when he recovers, he takes two blatant steps to manufacturing his own alcohol. The desire for alcohol, of course, is quite clearly forbidden by the fifth commandment so that has to be changed. Previously, the animals had been unable to detect how these changes have been made, and even now, with all the evidence of Squealer caught in the act, no one except Benjamin realises what is going on. Typically he will not tell the others.

Questions on Chapter Eight

1. Mention *two* ways in which Napoleon and Squealer control/distort information.
2. How does Napoleon display his love for personal glory?
3. How are the animals convinced that Snowball was a coward at the Battle of the Cowshed?
4. What is particularly significant about the public inspection of the bank-notes?
5. There are two reasons why the animals win the battle. What are they?
6. What is the purpose of the victory celebrations?
7. How many direct contradictions can you find in what Napoleon says and does?
8. How is it that the animals (excepting Benjamin) are unable to see that Squealer is rewriting the commandments?

Glossary

square: fit
meddle: interfere
violated: disregarded
retinue: group in attendance upon an important person
Crown Derby dinner service: complete, valuable set of plates and dishes for dinner (used by only Napoleon, to indicate his importance)
swill-bucket: container of pig food
surmounted: overtopped
skulking: hiding

impending: (something unpleasant) about to happen
magistrates: officials of the court
title-deeds: papers proving a person's right of ownership
of property
clamoured: demanded continually, loudly, strongly
tidings: news
machinations: plans for doing harm
nocturnal: at night-time
gander: male goose
privy: sharing secret knowledge of
hitherto: until that time
censured: blamed severely
in the teeth of: in opposition to
forsook: left
gambolled: jumped about in play
ecstasies: great joy and happiness
beatifically: peacefully happy
sentinels: guards
conciliatory: to win support
sallied: rushed out
refuge: shelter
unscathed: unharmed
detour: a way round something
flank: side
braced: prepared
hearse: the wagon used to carry the dead animals to
their funeral
lamentation: expression of grief or sorrow
contrived: skilfully planned

Chapter Nine

Boxer is sent to the knacker's yard.

Summary

Boxer, despite a split hoof, works as hard as ever as he looks forward to his retirement. Life is hard but Squealer is able to prove that things are much better than in Jones' day. He calls the reductions in rations "readjustments", and although they are often hungry and cold, the animals are convinced that they are better off, especially as they are free, not slaves.

Napoleon has fathered thirty-one young pigs who are raised separately from the other animals. They are to be educated in a proposed new schoolroom, but until then, Napoleon is to teach them himself. The pigs are granted more privileges.

The farm needs more money for purchases (e.g. the materials for the schoolroom) so more eggs are sold, rations reduced, oil saved. Yet the pigs seem to be putting on weight as they now drink the home-brewed beer. The animals are compensated for their hardships by diversions such as songs, speeches and processions. A "Spontaneous Demonstration" is ordered by Napoleon, once a week, to celebrate the struggles and the triumphs of Animal Farm. This helps the animals to forget, at least part of the time, that they are hungry.

Animal Farm is declared a Republic and Napoleon is elected President. Fresh evidence proves that Snowball was actually the leader of the human forces at the Battle of the Cowshed, and that the wound on his back was inflicted by Napoleon. Moses the raven reappears after several years' absence, and, unchanged, talks about the glories of Sugarcandy Mountain. The animals' lives are so hard that they are willing to believe him. The pigs, although contemptuous of his stories, allow him to stay, not working, and give him an allowance of beer.

Boxer's strength is failing, and he collapses through over-work. Napoleon arranges for Boxer to be taken to hospital in Willingdon. The animals are uneasy about this, as no animal, except for Mollie or Snowball, had ever left the farm. After a couple of days' rest for Boxer, Benjamin alerts the other animals that Boxer is being taken away by the Knacker (horse slaughterer). Despite their efforts, and Boxer's own feeble efforts to kick his way out of the van, he is taken away, and his death is announced three days later.

Squealer gives a sentimental account of Boxer's last words, his regret at passing away before the completion of the windmill, and his usual mottoes. Squealer explains away the rumour of Boxer going to the "Horse Slaughterer" by saying the van had been bought by the vet from the horse slaughterer, and the name had not yet been painted out. The animals believe this and feel relieved. Napoleon makes a speech praising Boxer and reminds the animals of Boxer's two favourite maxims.

Only the pigs take part in the memorial banquet for Boxer, getting drunk again on whisky.

Commentary

This chapter deals with the treatment of Boxer, as he battles on despite injuries, old age and declining strength. Despite his tremendous self-sacrifice, and his dream of retirement in the company of Benjamin, he is discarded, and sent to the knacker's yard as soon as his usefulness to the pigs is over. There he will be killed, used as dog meat, and his bones boiled to be used as glue. This shows how the pigs extract the maximum out of an individual, and give him nothing in return for a lifetime of devoted service. They might have gained much good publicity from an honourable treatment of Boxer in retirement, but they prefer to grab a bit of money from the knacker instead. Then they make up lies about Boxer's end to placate and inspire the other animals. Only Benjamin realises the true situation, but he is not a leader who can convince the animals. He leads the animals in attempting, unsuccessfully, to stop Boxer from being taken away, but he does not rebut Squealer's lies. Napoleon even exploits Boxer's murder to reinforce the two maxims — "I will work harder" and "Comrade Napoleon is always Right". The memorial banquet, enjoyed only by the pigs, is merely an excuse for depravity and drunkenness. The pigs not only drink alcohol, but drink to *excess*, therefore breaking even the amended commandment.

Boxer is very trusting, and it is touching to see how he believes in the promises of retirement comforts, when other promises are being broken, and rations constantly reduced (but not for the pigs). The small field reserved for retirement is not only taken away from the animals approaching retirement, but used to grow barley, solely for the benefit of the pigs.

The hardships are all explained away by Squealer, who is an adept manipulator, not only of statistics, but of language as well. For example, reductions in rations are always presented as "readjustments", and the inequality of the special treatment of the pigs and dogs is obscured by resorting to abstractions, like "Animalism".

Another way in which this unequality is reinforced is by the expense incurred in educating the young pigs. Not only are there many more of them (31), but they are to have a schoolhouse. No mention is now made of education for other animals as this might make them more difficult to control. The money for the building has to come from somewhere, and this is through reducing the living standards of the animals. It is squeezing the basic necessities of one group to provide luxuries for another small group — an elite — which is clearly contrary to the original ideals of equality. To get them to accept all this, the animals are distracted by entertainment and brainwashing. The irony of the "Spontaneous Demonstration" is that it is not spontaneous at all, but initiated by a "command" by Napoleon, and institutionalised to take place regularly according to a fixed pattern. However, despite some enjoyment, it does not really mask the basic problem — that they are hungry. Similarly, it is a joke that Napoleon becomes President, as it is unnecessary, and a farcical abuse of democracy, as there is only one candidate.

Further distortion and "revision" of Snowball's role in previous times now goes so far as to change him from the heroic leader of the animals, to the leader of the enemy. The gun shot wounds on his back are now supposed to have been inflicted by Napoleon, who was not even present at the Battle of the Cowshed.

Moses represents how religion is useful in getting the oppressed to accept present hardship for future happiness. He comes back because he is useful to the pigs, as he keeps many of the animals contented. He is rewarded for his role, being better fed (he has the luxury of beer) despite the fact that he does not work, whereas the animals have to work very hard indeed.

Benjamin displays his devotion to Boxer after his collapse, and it is this love that spurs Benjamin to positive action, rather than his characteristic passive cynicism. The pity is that Benjamin is intelligent, but does not communicate his insights to the other animals. Here, however, his love of Boxer inspires him to leadership, getting the animals to ignore the pig who is in charge, and fight to free Boxer. The point is, though, that it requires intelligence and collective action to right abuses, and the animals, who were stupidly just wishing Boxer farewell, have to have the situation explained to them. Even then, there is not complete unity, because the horses pulling the van are too stupid to realise what is going on.

Questions on Chapter Nine

1. How is the devotion of Clover and Benjamin to Boxer displayed?
2. What, according to Squealer, are "The Principles of Animalism"?
3. How do the conditions for the pigs improve, and how do conditions for other animals deteriorate?
4. What are the particular benefits of a belief in Sugarcandy Mountain?
5. Was it a good thing that Boxer was told of the true situation when he was being driven away? Give reasons to support your answer.
6. How do Squealer and Napoleon exploit the fact that only they know what really happened to Boxer after he left Animal Farm?
7. What is your opinion of Benjamin?

Glossary

poultices: hot, moist mixture of various substances spread on a cloth to lessen pain, swelling
superannuated: too old for work
piebald: coloured with black and white patches

wafted: carried

tureen: a large deep dish with a lid, from which soup is served at table

offset: made up for

precincts: enclosed area

complicity: partnership in wrongdoing (in this case, taking part with Jones in a crime)

strain: manner

professed: declared

prancing: moving quickly; springing about in a agitated manner

demeanour: outward manner

tempered: eased

oration: formal and solemn public speech

interment: burial

Chapter Ten

The pigs are more equal than others.

Summary

Years pass, many animals die, and few can remember the days before the rebellion. The retirement plan for animals has never been implemented, and whilst animals such as Clover suffer the effects of old age, Napoleon and Squealer get very fat. There are many more animals now, some brought in from outside Animal Farm, with little knowledge of the rebellion. The new horses are very stupid, and cannot understand what Clover tries to teach them about the rebellion and Animalism.

The farm is now more prosperous and enlarged, but the windmill, which was to have provided the animals with comfortable living quarters, (through electricity) is now used solely to produce cash profit. Napoleon denounces dreams of comfort (originated by Snowball), ironically claiming that "The truest happiness ... lay in working hard and living frugally".

The inequalities are obvious, but the animals do not realise it. Although the farm is prosperous, the animals are badly off, and they cannot remember pre-rebellion days. Anyway, Squealer is always proving, through statistics, that things are better. The pigs and the dogs, although they do not produce food themselves, live very comfortably. They claim to do vital paper work which ordinary animals are "too ignorant to understand". Benjamin knows what is going on, and can remember Jones' time, but he has a very gloomy outlook — "hunger, hardship and disappointment being ... the unalterable law of life".

Yet the animals are sustained by the traditions of the past,

their unique position of being the only farm in England wholly owned and operated by animals, and dreams of a future when all England would be free of humans. They still have the song, "Beasts of England" (sung in secret), to inspire them, their ideal of equality, and the comfort that all their hard work is for their own benefit.

The animals are then shattered by two successive shocks — the first is the sight of the pigs walking on two legs, and then of Napoleon carrying a whip. This is so extreme that the animals are just about to protest when they are drowned by the new bleat of the sheep — "Four legs good, two legs better!" Squealer had prepared for this moment by spending a whole week teaching them this new slogan.

Clover is alert enough to check the seven commandments, but Benjamin is able to read for her that the seven commandments have now been reduced to one: "All animals are equal, but some animals are more equal than others."

Now all the pigs use whips when supervising the animals at work, and the pigs adopt all the habits and luxuries of humans. Neighbouring farmers are shown round, and are much impressed, especially by the windmill. The animals are greatly confused, not knowing whether to fear the pigs or the humans more. The leading pigs entertain the farmers to drinks and a game of cards. Pilkington makes a speech in which he praises the discipline and efficiency of the farm, especially the fact that the "lower animals ... did more work and received less food than any animals in the county". He says that all human fears of a farm owned and operated by pigs have been proved wrong. He identifies with the pigs — they have trouble with their lower animals, just as humans have trouble with their lower classes. Napoleon replies by saying that he is glad the misunderstanding is over, that the pigs have no intention of promoting revolution on neighbouring farms. He claims that the farm is "a cooperative enterprise ... owned by the pigs jointly" (note that he excludes the other animals). He announces several major changes: abolishing the term "Comrade", paying respect to Major's skull on Sunday mornings, and the removal of the hoof and horn from the flag. The most significant change is that Animal Farm will henceforth be known by its previous name of Manor Farm. To the animals peeping in from outside, the appearance of the pigs seems to be changing. Then, after a row over cheating at cards, pigs and humans look, sound and behave exactly the same. The animals can no longer tell the difference.

Commentary

In this chapter, we see the ideals and new traditions of the rebellion destroyed, while the pigs adopt the ways of the humans completely. The process of gradually assuming more power, and adopting a lifestyle contrary to that suggested by Major, is now complete. So the betrayal is now complete — instead of being tyrannised by humans, the animals are tyrannised by the pigs, whose only wish is for power and privilege. Everything that the original rebellion stood for — equality, mutual help and protection, rejection of the corrupt lifestyle of humans — is now destroyed, and the outcome is that the animals are unable to distinguish between humans and pigs. They are now back to their original position of fearful obedience to a cruel and exploitative master. In addition, they are stripped of their illusions, most especially their belief that all their efforts and suffering are for the common good, not to sustain a small band of rulers in unfair luxury.

One of the great problems for the animals lies in their poor memory, and because of this, they become passive, and are easily cheated by the pigs. This is shown in how the traditions of the rebellion are lost, how the new generation can hardly remember the reasons, the ideals, of the original rebellion. The fact is the rich get richer and the poor get poorer. The pigs get fatter, and the promises to the animals (such as the retirement plan) are broken. The farm is more prosperous, so there ought to be improvements for all — they have more land, the power of the windmill, more machinery and better know-how. The inspiration given to the animals by Snowball was that of a better life, easier and more comfortable. Napoleon, however, exploits the idealism of the animals, urging them to a saintly life of self-denial — which leaves more of the farm's wealth for the exclusive benefit of the pigs, and the dogs that sustain them in power by brute force. These groups are increasing in numbers, which of course means that they consume more. The animals cannot check on living standards, because they have no valid means of comparison. Only Benjamin can remember, but he is so cynical that he never believed in the idealism of the revolution in the first place, so he does not expect that life can be improved anyway.

The animals are sustained, not so much by Squealer's false figures (which conceal the fact that the pigs must be taking more than Jones and his men in their day, because the farm is producing more, but the other animals are eating less and working harder), but by dreams — of the past, present and future. The waking dream of the present is that they are independent, regulating their own affairs. The dream of the past is the heroic battles, and the dream of the future is the spread of the ideals of animal equality and the defeat of humans throughout England (representing the spread of Communism outside Russia to the rest of the world).

The heart of the matter is that most creatures (people)

are not saints, and the survival of the banned song, "Beasts of England", shows that they need an ideal world to dream of. Napoleon's definition of true happiness — hard work and suffering — is not convincing. It also shows the universal truth that you can suppress aspirations, but you cannot kill them.

The irony is that the animals co-operate in their own enslavement. The sheep, for example, are unable to see that "two legs better" is a direct contradiction of the truth.

The chapter begins with a calm review of the events, and this long period of quiet highlights the shock of Clover seeing Squealer walking on two legs. This sentence (p.113), like the one about Napoleon carrying a whip (p.117), is given maximum impact by being short, without any decoration, and highlighted by being printed on a separate line as a paragraph on its own. This helps to give the shock time to hit and to sink in. The following sentence — "there was a deadly silence" (p.113) — shows that this is an important, critical climax. The animals have been tricked into accepting numerous "revisions" of the commandments, but this is too blatant to ignore. Despite the whip, the dogs, their long habit of never complaining, an explosion of protest is just about to take place, when it is prevented by the bleating of the sheep. The pigs have been smart enough to prepare for this moment by getting a stupid majority to drown out the more sensible minority. The other aspect of this stage-managed sudden grab of power (sometimes called a 'coup' and stage-managed in the sense of careful preparation and timing) is that the pigs quickly get out of the way.

Clover knows that the key to its morality must be in the commandments, and the finality of what is now there is savage. All the original, detailed rules are gone, except for the cynical distortion of the final one, which is clearly contradictory, since "equal" is an absolute — you are either equal or not equal, you cannot be "more equal".

Orwell does not dwell on this much, except in showing further corruption by the pigs in absurd details of human habits, and the clear distinction of the "more equal animals" by the power of their whips. However, the statement itself is graphically highlighted by the way it is printed on the page. This is the central message of his book, and this is a way of making it memorable. The discovery could have been accompanied by anger or outrage, but the effect is tinted by pathos, because of the description of the cruelly deceived Clover. She is intelligent enough (just) to know what is happening, after a lifetime of self-sacrifice, disappointment and suffering. She is gentle in her movements, rather than agitated, and she makes no fuss at this crisis. "Her old eyes looked dimmer than ever", as if realising that all of her illusions are about to be shattered.

The visit of the farmers is another satirical dig at how the better features of the farm are highlighted, but this time (in contrast to how Whymper was deceived into telling the outside world that there was no food shortage on Animal Farm) the farmers are told that the prosperity of the farm depends on more work and less food for the animals. (This represents the way in which the Rapid Industrialisation of Russia was achieved, to the amazement of the outside world, but by brutal methods.)

Pilkington's speech shows the hypocrisy of those who have only self-interest at heart. They will say or do anything, break any promise, compromise on principle, shake hands with an enemy, in order to maintain privilege. What was formerly seen as a contest between humans and animals — groups with fundamentally different interests — is now seen as a contest between masters (humans and pigs) and slaves (the other animals and the lower classes). This puts the classic Trotskyist (Snowball) position in perspective — that revolution must be international, and it is not a case of war between nations, but war between classes, the workers and the rulers. As Pilkington states, "between pigs and human beings there was not, and there need not be, any clash of interests whatever". He recognises that the "success" of Animal Farm is based on exploitation of the other animals, for which he congratulates the pigs.

Napoleon's reply is that the pigs have never intended, as rumoured, to "export revolution" to neighbouring farms, and sees mutual self-interest in maintaining friendly relations with neighbours in terms of trade and security. Without knowing that the other animals are listening in, he announces that the farm is owned by the pigs only, which makes a mockery of the term "cooperative enterprise" (this means that *everyone* who works in the group has joint ownership, and an equal right to decide policy). For the purpose of proving to the humans that there will be no more worry about rebellion, he announces the abolition of three things, all significant. The term "comrade" is abolished because it indicates equality, an ideal that the ruling class (humans and pigs) do not want to encourage. Neither does Napoleon want the ideas of Major to survive, so the custom of honouring his memory by the Sunday morning march past is also abolished. The hoof and horn, which symbolise the unity of all animals *against* humans, are removed (The hammer and sickle on the Russian flag represent industrial and agricultural workers united against a ruling class.)

The final blow to the animals' dream is the removal of the word "animal" from the name of the Farm. For a long time, it had only been an illusion that the animals controlled their own destiny, but now the reality is that the pigs are more like humans than animals, and have betrayed their old comrades for new friends, who were once their former enemies. The change of name has the dual purpose of cementing relationships with the humans — going back to a human name means accepting human values — and showing that the pigs have complete control, so much so that they no longer need to feed the animals dreams of owning their own farm.

The conclusion is a row in which the pigs and humans are indistinguishable, and whatever the outcome, we know, and the animals now realise, that it cannot be good for them — the truth is that they are in a worse position than before, betrayed and exploited by their own kind, and with no effective leaders to turn to. The message seems to be that every abuse of power, however small, must be met with firm resistance, and that every ideal and principle, must be jealously guarded. Trusting in others to make decisions, not having the courage to question and fight, will only lead to abuse and exploitation. Since the animals are, in fact, representing human nature, Orwell is suggesting that human nature is selfish, and that power corrupts (that is, you use power just for your personal advantage, not for the general good). While the struggles of the working class are seen as heroic and noble, they are built on the false promise that their leaders will remain true to the original, shared ideals.

It has been suggested that George Orwell was a pessimist (sharing the views of Benjamin, so much so that he was known to his friends as "Donkey George") offering no answer to this gloomy view of human nature. Whether this is true, or whether the solution hinted at above (that the price of liberty is eternal vigilance, that Government can be controlled by an active and politically aware population) is for the reader to decide.

Questions on Chapter Ten

1. Why is it that Boxer, for all his superb contribution, is now forgotten?
2. What phrase suggests that the second windmill will not be used for the benefit of all the animals?
3. Why is Benjamin such a disappointment?
4. Had "the early days of the rebellion, when Jones' expulsion was still recent", been a brief golden age? If so, how?
5. Are the animals to be admired, or pitied, for never giving up hope?
6. How many climaxes are there in the second half of the chapter?
7. The pigs and humans meet "on terms of equality". Why is it that the pigs conform to the human habits, and not the other way round? (Remember how the animals were impressed by Napoleon on four legs giving orders to Whymper on two.)

Glossary

inebriates' home: home for those who are habitually drunk
rheumy: watering
morose: gloomy, not speaking
taciturn: speaking little; silent
denounced: spoke against
frugally: not wastefully; sparingly
trifle: slightly
haughty: proud
nuzzling: rubbing with nose
wireless set: old name for radio
subscriptions: amount of money paid regularly in order to receive the magazines and newspapers

ratcatcher breeches: trousers fastened at the knee (to prevent rats running up the trouser leg)

leggings: outer covering of leather worn to protect the legs, especially from foot to knee

deputation: group appointed to represent others

incumbent: having a moral duty

current: passing from one person to another; generally accepted as true or genuine

licence: uncontrolled behaviour

subsisted: were kept alive

bon mot: a clever saying, joke (French)

intimated: suggested

subversive: destructive

suppressed: crushed by force

emptied to the dregs: drunk to the last drop

CHARACTERS

Major

Old Major is the inspiration of the rebellion. He analyses clearly how man exploits animals and gives the animals a vision of the future: "A dream of the earth as it will be when man has vanished" (p.12). He composes a song, "Beasts of England", which inspires, unifies and motivates the animals. But most important of all, he lays down the principles of Animalism, such as: "In fighting against Man, we must not come to resemble him. Even when you have conquered him, do not adopt his vices ... And above all, no animal must ever tyrannize over his own kind. Weak or strong, clever or simple, we are all brothers" (p.12). This is the stirring message that inspires the animals to rebel, to resist counter-attack, and to endure extreme hardship. It is the vision that Clover and the other animals long for after the mass executions (pp.75-6).

Major is a good speaker, able to focus his argument clearly for the animals by posing key rhetorical questions and simple statements, with much gory detail, and repetition for emphasis. Examples of rhetorical questions (that is, questions to which the answers are obvious, but have an emotional effect on the audience) are: "What have you ever had except your bare rations and a stall?" (p.9) and "Is it not crystal clear, then, comrades, that all the evils of this life of ours spring from the tyranny of human beings?" (p.10). Examples of simple statements: "Let us face it: our lives are miserable, laborious and short" (p.8) and "Man is the only creature that consumes without producing" (p.9). Gory detail: "Every one of you will scream your life out at the block within a year" (p.10). His use of repetition is very effective in clarifying the problem: "There comrades, is the answer to all our problems. It is summed up in a single word — *Man*. *Man* is the only real enemy we have. Remove *Man* from the scene, and the root cause of hunger and over-work is abolished forever" (p.9).

I have dwelt on Major's speaking skills because they are important. Often the potential for revolution is there, but it needs a focus, and this is usually a leader who can put into words what the others are thinking and feeling. Major communicates well, and gives the animals values (e.g. all animals are equal) which are simple to understand and remember. He also provides them with the song which gives them hope, unity and pride in themselves. Unfortunately, there is one flaw in his argument, which is that if Man is removed, all will be well. If he had said remove tyranny, he would have been right, but he could not imagine that animals would turn against each other.

Major is representative of Lenin, the brain and shining light of the Russian Revolution of 1917. All the others, including Stalin (Napoleon) and Trotsky (Snowball), respected and were loyal to him, but unfortunately he suffered strokes and died too early. We can only speculate what would have happened if he had lived and been able to exert his wise will on the others. However, this is the political, serious aspect. The "fairy story" treatment makes Major somewhat lenient and lovable — "I ... have had over four hundred children. Such is the natural life of a pig" (p.10). He is well-respected: "So highly regarded on the farm that everyone was quite ready to lose an hour's sleep in order to hear what he had to say" (p.5). He commands respect because of his age, his appearance, his dignity, but most of all, his wisdom: "He was twelve years old and lately grown rather stout, but he was still a majestic-looking pig, with a wise and benevolent appearance" (pp.5-6). He is benevolent because he is concerned about the welfare of others, not himself — his own life is very comfortable: "I am one of the lucky ones" (p.10).

Without Major, there would have been no rebellion.

Key Points

1. Wise
2. Good speaker
3. Altruistic (wanting the good of others)
4. Commands respect
5. Inspiring
6. Imposing appearance

Key Quotes

1. "The whole of the produce of our labour is stolen from us by human beings" (p.8).
2. "Let us face it: our lives are miserable, laborious and short" (p.8).
3. "For myself, I do not grumble, for I am one of the luck ones" (p.10).
4. "So highly regarded on the farm that everyone was quite ready to lose an hour's sleep in order to hear what he had to say" (p.5).
5. "The singing of this song threw the animals into the wildest excitement. Almost before Major had reached the end, they had begun singing it themselves" (p.14).
6. "A majestic-looking pig, with a wise and benevolent appearance" (pp.5-6).

Napoleon

Napoleon is "a large, rather fierce-looking Berkshire boar ... not much of a talker, but with a reputation for getting his own way" (p.15).

He is a ruthless dictator, solely concerned with his own power and comfort. He achieves this by any means possible, including mass murder, starvation, lies and the re-writing of history to turn heroes like Snowball into villains. He sinks so low that even a worthy hero like Boxer is killed for profit as soon as he is no longer useful.

How does Napoleon achieve his aims? One, by force — the use of the fierce dogs (army, or secret police) to silence opposition, and also to protect him. Two, by controlling information, mainly through Squealer, to discredit opponents like Snowball, to destroy the traditions and ideals of old Major, and to falsify the living conditions of the animals. Three, by bewildering switches of policy, planned and executed with astonishing speed and decisiveness. Four, by manipulating the stupid sheep to bleat, "Four legs good, two legs bad" (or even worse, "Four legs good, two legs better") every time any discussion unfavourable to Napoleon is likely. Five, by working behind the scenes to ensure that the more stupid animals will always vote for him, regardless of any arguments they might hear.

He has undoubted leadership ability. He is astute, intelligent, single-minded, and he knows how to exploit the weaknesses in others; he plays on their fears, ignorance and stupidity. He and Snowball are the natural leaders during the early part of the rebellion. Together with Squealer, they work out the Seven Commandments which incorporate the basic principles of Animalism.

Recognising that simple animals need simple arguments, he uses Squealer to reduce complex issues to easily remembered slogans such as "Four legs good, two legs bad" and later, when it suits his purposes, "Four legs good, two legs better!"

He is not prepared to share in physical toil or hardship (does not help in the harvesting). Neither is he prepared to share the fruits of the animals' labour. (The milk and apples are for the pigs only.)

Knowledge is power, so Napoleon keeps the other animals in ignorance while the pigs learn useful skills. Unlike Snowball, he does not believe in educating the masses. In Chapter Nine, the thirty-one young pigs (his children) are to have the privilege of separate education in a specially built schoolroom. Meanwhile, Napoleon instructs them.

Napoleon's competition with Snowball reveals his short-term outlook, compared to Snowball's wider vision of a much improved, cultured future life for all the animals. Napoleon can only think of immediate needs, such as food and alcohol. Similarly, he sees the problem of defending the farm within the narrow framework of a battle, whereas Snowball sees their long-term security in spreading the rebellion outside to other animals.

Perhaps Napoleon is just argumentative, instinctively opposing anyone else's ideas. He scorns Snowball's plan for the windmill, but in an astonishing turnabout, he later decides in favour of it.

He will brook no opposition, and his rivalry with Snowball starts early. The defeat of Snowball is achieved by great cunning; it is completely unexpected. The animals expect the dispute over the windmill to be settled by speeches and a democratic vote. Instead, Napoleon looses his dogs on Snowball in a brilliant *coup*, theatrical and spectacular, which leaves the animals "silent and terrified" (p.48).

With Snowball removed, Napoleon dismantles the apparatus of democracy so that free speech will no longer hinder him. He does this in his usual way, through force and brainwashing. (Orwell calls this "Thought Control" in a later book, *1984*.) The dogs frighten the young porkers who are intelligent enough to be an effective opposition, and Squealer distorts the case for Napoleon ("he would be only too happy to let you make decisions for yourselves", p.50) and against Snowball ("No better than a criminal", p.50). The use of a scapegoat (Snowball) and a scare story (Jones coming back) become standard techniques to confuse the issue.

Napoleon is fond of startling actions and announcements, which are immediate and final, backed up with the "friendly persuasion" of his terrifying dogs. He does not believe in discussion before any decision, but relies on surprise and subsequent brainwashing.

His force of personality and power inspire blind devotion ("Napoleon is always right," says Boxer) and he exploits this to the full. The other animals are urged to adopt Boxer's motto. However, even Boxer is attacked by the dogs when he tries to defend Snowball.

Napoleon distances himself from the other animals, even the pigs. With his special security guards (the dogs) and a personal food taster, he trusts no one.

Without conscience or morals, he has the means to do whatever he wants. If it suits him to change the Commandments, he does so. If he goes back on previous attitudes or decisions (about the windmill, Snowball, Pilkington, or Frederick), he just twists the facts. His hypocrisy is passed off as "cunning". For example, Squealer claims that the windmill was originally Napoleon's idea and he had merely "*seemed* to oppose" it.

Like all despots, Napoleon not only enjoys exercising power, but he enjoys the trappings of power. The only boar on the farm, he has all four females to himself. He awards himself medals, has his birthday celebrated as a "National" event, lives sumptuously, names the windmill after himself, makes himself President, and starts a personality cult in which he has "the credit for every successful achievement and every stroke of good fortune" (p.80).

Under him, brainwashing is total: the past is rubbed out ("Beasts of England", the flag, old Major's skull and the Seven Commandments) and replaced by Napoleon's image, in words and painting.

Understanding mob psychology, he leaks stories out to play on the emotions of the masses (e.g. that Frederick had "killed a dog by throwing it in the furnace", p.82; and that "Comrade Napoleon was dying", p.92). He distracts the animals from the truth and their misery by Celebrations (of their hollow victory), by Spontaneous Demonstrations, by meetings (even when their part is merely to receive orders and sing the song). He knows the value of words in brainwashing, the effectiveness of slogans, titles ("Terror of Mankind", p.79), songs and poems. He knows a mob can be easily roused, easily frightened (by details of Snowball's alleged plots and the threat of Jones coming back). He knows the value of a public spectacle (the confessions and mass executions — "A pile of corpses lying before Napoleon's feet and the air was heavy with the smell of blood", p.74).

He dominates other animals and manages, amazingly, to distort a whole philosophy of equality and cooperation into its very opposite — privilege for the few at the expense of the majority.

Although he can at times be outwitted, and appear ridiculous because of his vanity, he is greatly to be feared for his ruthless ability to impose his will on everyone else. Old Major is the star of Chapter One; Snowball shares the stage from Chapters Two to Five; but Napoleon dominates the rest of the book.

Key Points

1. General description: large, fierce, silent, determined
2. Ruthless — eliminates opposition
3. Has leadership ability
4. Is lazy, corrupt and vain
5. Has only a short term outlook
6. A brilliant political tactician
7. Completely dictatorial: opposes anyone else's ideas, brooks no opposition, rules by terror and force
8. Aloof
9. Enjoys the trappings of power
10. Destroys all the principles of Animalism
11. Understands the masses
12. Dominates the story

Key Quotes

1. "Not much of a talker, but with a reputation for getting his own way" (p.15)
2. "The superior quality of Napoleon's mind, said Squealer, was shown in the fact that he trusted nobody, not even Frederick" (p.85).
3. "He had *seemed* to oppose the windmill, simply as a manoeuvre to get rid of Snowball" (p.52).
4. "For he had recently awarded himself 'Animal Hero, First Class', and 'Animal Hero, Second Class'" (p.72).
5. "But by and large the animals enjoyed these celebrations. They found it comforting to be reminded that, after all, they were truly their own masters and that the work they did was for their own benefit" (p.98).

6. "When they had finished their confession, the dogs promptly tore their throats out" (p.73).
7. "All questions relating to the working of the farm would be settled by a special committee of pigs, presided over by himself" (p.49).
8. "He suddenly roared in a voice of thunder" (p.62).
9. "Terror of Mankind" (p.79).

Snowball

"Snowball was a more vivacious pig than Napoleon, quicker in speech and more inventive, but was not considered to have the same depth of character" (p.15).

Because of his eloquence and lively personality, Snowball is good at putting ideas across to the masses. He is intelligent enough to reduce all the principles of Animalism to a single maxim, "Four legs good, two legs bad." Although his explanation of how this affects the birds is sophistry, he is able to convince them. The inventiveness of his imagination is shown in both the long-term vision of a golden age ("In glowing sentences he painted a picture of Animal Farm as it might be when sordid labour was lifted from the animals' backs", p.47) and in practical detail ("Snowball's plans for the windmill were fully worked out", p.44).

"Not considered to have the same depth of character" is not really a fair comparison, because Snowball is open (extrovert) and reveals himself and his thoughts, while Napoleon is secretive (introvert), more of an unknown quality, and therefore thought to be "deep".

Snowball is intellectual, eloquent, brave, enthusiastic, and a natural leader. He may not be as incorruptible as his name suggests (purity of snow). After all, he approves of the pigs' exclusive right to the apples and milk — "All the pigs were in full agreement on this point, even Snowball and

Napoleon" (p.32). But in general, his character and outlook are much more positive than Napoleon's.

Perhaps Snowball is more of a visionary, with a long-term view, whereas Napoleon is more pragmatic, more interested in safeguarding immediate gains. They disagree on two major points of policy. (1) Industrialisation: Snowball advocates the building of the windmill, which will provide a three-day week, electric light, warmth and comfort for all the animals; but this will mean less food for a while, as building will take priority over food production. (2) Defence: Snowball sees that in the long-term Animal Farm will always be under siege, as it is the only farm run by animals. He advocates spreading revolution to other farms as the best means of defence — "If rebellions happened everywhere they would have no need to defend themselves" (p.46).

His intellect is vast; he reads widely and his futuristic concepts ("Snowball conjured up pictures of fantastic machines which would do their work for them", p.44) are backed up with hard, detailed work. Sometimes his schemes are rather idealistic and impractical, such as the Whiter Wool Movement for the sheep and the Wild Comrades Re-education Committee. Nevertheless, Snowball's energy and enthusiasm ("He was indefatigable", p.29) are admirable.

Snowball's originality is revealed not only in his successful motivation and organisation of the animals, but in his attempts at modernisation and his clever turning of abstractions, like freedom, into intelligible symbols, like the flag (p.28).

Like Napoleon, he is competitive; he always opposes Napoleon in the debates. However, he is not as cunning a tactician as Napoleon, and his eloquence ("Snowball often won over the majority by his brilliant speeches", p.43) is defeated by Napoleon's practical methods of canvassing support, his arranged interruptions of Snowball's speeches and his use of terror. Maybe Snowball wants too much too soon, and would have been more successful, and survived, if he had proceeded more cautiously. ("Napoleon produced no schemes of his own, but said quietly that Snowball's would come to nothing, and seemed to be biding his time", p.43).

There is no doubt about Snowball's leadership ability; he produces ideas, organises practical work, finds solutions, leads the defence of the farm by clever strategy and personal bravery. But he is defeated by Napoleon because he has not secured his power base. Although generally popular, he has no group with blind obedience to him, as Napoleon has in the dogs and sheep. He lacks this basic understanding of the stupidity and selfishness that can be exploited by crude power. While Snowball is enjoying himself in the public limelight, Napoleon is doing his homework with his dogs and sheep. Snowball is perhaps too much of an intellectual to get down to the basic level of self-protection.

He leads well in peace and war. He organises the harvest ("Comrade Snowball will lead the way", p.24). In the Battle of the Cowshed he is associated with the great soldier, Julius Caesar, outwits the humans and shows outstanding courage. His award of "Animal Hero, First Class" is thoroughly deserved, and it is awarded by the admiring animals. Compare this to Napoleon's awards to himself, for no achievements in particular.

After Snowball's expulsion from Animal Farm, Napoleon gives Squealer the task of destroying Snowball's reputation. Immediately, he is branded "a criminal" (p.50) and his bravery cast into doubt. This is the first step in a gradual process in convincing the animals of Snowball's villainy.

The pigs spread lies about his movements and set about denigrating his enormous contribution to the success of Animal Farm. This can be illustrated by the windmill. Snowball's brainchild ("moonshine", according to Squealer) is suddenly adopted by Napoleon, who had previously been very much against it. Then Squealer reveals that Snowball had stolen the plan from Napoleon ("the windmill was, in fact, Napoleon's own creation", p.52).

Another way in which Snowball's role in history is completely re-written is the changed account of the Battle of the Cowshed. From being its great hero, Snowball's role is gradually debased ("The time will come when we shall find that Snowball's part in it was much exaggerated", p.50). Then he was accused of being an agent of Jones (p.71); and finally the animals are told that "Snowball had not, as the animals had previously imagined, merely attempted to lose the Battle of the Cowshed by means of a stratagem, but had actually been the leader of the human forces" (p.99).

We can only assess Snowball's role accurately up to Chapter Five, when he is chased out. There is no evidence of what he does in exile, other than the claims made by the pigs. Unfortunately, the animals have short memories and believe anything they are told. Boxer's attempt to defend Snowball ("I do not believe that Snowball was a traitor at the beginning", p.71) is suppressed. Snowball is held responsible for the destruction of the windmill, which was actually a natural disaster, and every trivial thing that goes wrong. The animals are so brainwashed that the cows swear that he is milking them in their sleep (p.86). Every troublesome group, like the rats, is said to be plotting with Snowball. "It seemed to them as though Snowball was some kind of invisible influence, pervading the air about them and menacing them with all kinds of dangers" (p.69). The big scare story is that he is to help Frederick to recapture the farm. With the passage of time, the pigs are able to change completely the truth of Snowball's life, since few can remember. Even if they could, they are confused by "fresh documents" (p.99), or too scared to speak up.

Snowball's role is that of someone of great talent, vision and energy whose place is at the beginning of momentous change. Once the change has been started, he is not ruthless enough to survive against those who will use any means to grab power for its own sake. Snowball may not have been a complete idealist, but he did try to make life better for all the animals, and he deserved some recognition and praise.

Key Points

1. Brilliant speaker
2. Far-sighted; visionary
3. Inventive
4. Brave
5. Good leader and strategist
6. Argumentative, egotistical
7. Partly corrupt
8. Good organiser, but impractical at times
9. Attractive extrovert personality
10. Energetic and enthusiastic
11. Unsentimental

Key Quotes

1. "Snowball often won over the majority by his brilliant speeches" (p.43).
2. "The luxuries of which Snowball had once taught the animals to dream, the stalls with electric light and hot and cold water, and the three-day week" (p.109).

3. "Snowball conjured up pictures of fantastic machines that would do their work for them" (p.44).

4. "Snowball fought bravely at the Battle of the Cowshed" (Boxer, p.70).

5. "He rallied and encouraged them at every turn" (p.70); "Snowball ... had studied an old book of Julius Caesar's campaigns" (p.37).

6. "As usual, Snowball and Napoleon were in disagreement" (p.46).

7. About the apples: "All the pigs were in full agreement on this point, even Snowball and Napoleon" (p.32).

8. "Snowball also busied himself with organizing the other animals into what he called Animal Committees ... On the whole, these projects were a failure" (p.29).

9. "Snowball was a more vivacious pig than Napoleon, quicker in speech and more inventive" (p.15).

10. "He was indefatigable in this" (p.29); "Now, comrades, said Snowball ... to the hayfield! Let us make it a point of honour to get in the harvest more quickly than Jones and his men could do" (p.24).

11. "War is war. The only good human being is a dead one" (p.39).

Squealer

"He was a brilliant talker, and when he was arguing some difficult point he had a way of skipping from side to side and whisking his tale which was somehow very persuasive. The others said of Squealer that he could turn black into white" (p.16).

Squealer becomes the agent and mouthpiece of Napoleon, probably because of Napoleon's greater physical power (Napoleon was "a large, rather fierce-looking Berkshire

Boar''; Squealer is a small fat porker, a castrated pig. Castrated animals lose their aggression). Another probable reason is that Squealer recognises that Napoleon is able and ruthless enough to become a dictator, and he wants to benefit, and survive, by being completely loyal and useful to Napoleon. As far as we can see, he has no conscience to trouble him.

Squealer's name is unattractive, as is his appearance, and it suggests not only his shrill voice, but a tendency to whine and tell lies — ''to squeal'' — or to inform, to spy or reveal something said in confidence. Squealer's job is to present the policies and actions of Napoleon's ruling class, the pigs, in a favourable light.

Napoleon is not much of a talker himself, and he leaves this important aspect to the carefully chosen and gifted Squealer. Abrupt changes in policy are part of Napoleon's style, and he does not give any reasons for changing his mind. In the case of the windmill, Squealer's job is to explain Napoleon's great cunning in pretending to oppose Snowball's plan, and he makes the barefaced claim that it was Napoleon's own plan, stolen by Snowball. Despite the facts, Squealer is able to convince the animals by a combination of deliberate intellectual confusion, charm, and force. (''He repeated a number of times, 'Tactics, comrades, tactics!' skipping round and whisking his tail with a merry laugh. The animals were not certain what the word meant, but Squealer spoke so persuasively, and the three dogs who happened to be with him growled so threateningly, that they accepted his explanation without further questions'', p.52).

Notice (1) The confusion — the animals do not know or understand the word tactics, but Squealer ''repeated it a number of times''. Repetition has a way of numbing the brain into acceptance. (2) The charm — although ugly,

Squealer has some attractive mannerisms, (like nimble movements, a readiness to laugh, and a whisking tail) essential to salesmanship. (3) The force — the three dogs "who happened to be with him" are not there by chance, as suggested by the words "happened to be". They are there in a deliberate move to ensure acceptance of Squealer's explanation.

However, Squealer's charm is very superficial. When crossed, he can use threats, and reveals his anger in the way he speaks so deliberately to Boxer. "Speaking very slowly and firmly", he announces that Napoleon "has stated categorically — categorically, comrade — that Snowball was Jones's agent from the very beginning" (p.71). Even after Boxer accepts this explanation, Squealer casts "a very ugly look at Boxer with his little twinkling eyes" (p.71). The "twinkling eyes" reveal, not a friendly attitude, but a sharp, evil intelligence at work.

Squealer is a master of language, and skilled at twisting it. It is reasonable to assume that he wrote the speech for Napoleon which announced work on Sunday afternoons as being "strictly voluntary, but any animal who absented himself from it would have his rations cut by half" (p.53). This kind of "doublethink" comes easily to someone who is in control of information, and can "turn black into white". He produces statistics to prove the increased production of food, and "The animals saw no reason to disbelieve him", but "would sooner have had less figures and more food" (p.79).

Squealer can turn a loss (of the windmill) into a victory, and a hero (Snowball) into a villain. He is clever enough to join with Napoleon and Snowball in writing the principles of Animalism (p.16), and cunning enough not to cross Napoleon or become over-ambitious. He prospers and becomes "so fat that he could with difficulty see out of his eyes" (p.108). Another way in which he ensures his own safety is to avoid danger: he "had unaccountably been absent during the fighting" (p.90). He is trusted enough by Napoleon to issue orders. "All orders were now issued through Squealer or one of the other pigs" (p.79). Other than direct orders and "explanations" of policy, Squealer's other methods include rumours and scare stories — "It was given out that Napoleon had arranged to sell the pile of timber to Mr Pilkington" (p.82). This is not an official announcement, but a rumour to keep Frederick and the animals guessing.

The rumours about Snowball vary to suit the current negotiating position of the pigs — he is supposed to be either with Frederick or Pilkington. Snowball is the scapegoat for everything going wrong, and the spectre of Jones is used to silence any opposition — "Surely none of you wishes to see Jones back?" (p.60). Squealer is also adept at organising the masses, especially the sheep, and is even able to put across the bewildering change from "Four legs good, two legs bad" (p.31) to "Four legs good, two legs better!" (p.114).

Of course anyone who is constantly telling lies must be a good actor. The pack of lies he tells about Boxer's murder is full of convincing detail (Boxer's last words, the expensive medicines, etc.) and false emotion ("Said Squealer, lifting his trotter and wiping away a tear", p.105). He is a complete hypocrite.

The worst crime in which Squealer takes a major part (no doubt because of his ability to manipulate language) is in the re-writing of the Seven Commandments, and he is actually caught in the act, but only Benjamin can understand what he is up to. Careful to protect himself, he is a shameless flatterer of Napoleon, painting his portrait on the barn, and promoting the hero-worship through titles, poems, songs and ceremonies.

Even without Napoleon's personal fierceness and mega-lomania, Squealer is just as wicked, as he abuses his gifts for evil purposes.

Key Points

1. Brilliant speaker
2. Very persuasive and charming
3. Good actor
4. Vindictive
5. Coward
6. Dependent on Napoleon
7. Re-writes the Commandments
8. Self-indulgent

Key Quotes

1. "A brilliant talker, ... he could turn black into white" (p.16).
2. "He repeated a number of times, 'Tactics, comrades, tactics!' skipping round and whisking his tail with a merry laugh. The animals were not certain what the word meant, but Squealer spoke so persuasively ... that they accepted his explanation" (p.52).
3. "It was the most affecting sight I have ever seen!' said Squealer, lifting his trotter and wiping away a tear" (p.105).
4. "He cast a very ugly look at Boxer with his little twinkling eyes" (p.71).
5. "Squealer ... had unaccountably been absent from the fighting" (p.90).

6. "A portrait of Napoleon, in profile, executed by Squealer in white paint" (p.81).
7. "Where the Seven Commandments were written, there lay a ladder broken in two pieces. Squealer, temporarily stunned, was sprawling beside it, and near at hand there lay a lantern, a paint brush, and an overturned pot of white paint" (p.93).
8. "Squealer was so fat that he could with difficulty see out of his eyes" (p.108)

Boxer

Boxer is the hero and victim of the novel. Hard-working, generous and self-sacrificing to a fault, he lacks intelligence and therefore his blind obedience to a corrupt leader, Napoleon, is cruelly exploited. Brave both physically (the battles with the humans) and morally (in standing up to Squealer and insisting that "Snowball fought bravely at the Battle of the Cowshed ... I saw him myself", p.70), Boxer deserves much better than to be tossed aside as soon as his usefulness to the pigs is over.

Boxer has many virtues, and only one weakness — his gullibility. He is easily exploited and manipulated by Napoleon, probably because he believes in obeying authority and thinking that a leader must be completely trustworthy. Having decided that he is too easily confused by arguments, he has simplified his life to the motto "Napoleon is always right" (p.50). Boxer makes a fundamental mistake in assuming that because Napoleon *ought* to be "always right", he actually *is* always right. The reality is that Napoleon is not, and to a certain extent it is Boxer's own fault that leads to his exploitation and death.

Boxer has a wonderful character. "He was not of first-rate intelligence, but he was universally respected for his steadiness of character and tremendous powers of work" (p.6). His very first act shows his caring nature: "Boxer and Clover came in together, walking very slowly and setting down their vast hairy hoofs with great care lest there should be some small animal concealed in the straw" (p.6). Even towards enemies, he is very generous, as when he thinks he has killed a stable-lad: "He is dead,' said Boxer sorrowfully. 'I had no intention of doing that ... Who will believe that I did not do this on purpose?" (p.39). Even when attacked by the dogs, Boxer does not exploit his great strength: "Boxer looked at Napoleon to know whether he should crush the dog to death or let it go" (p.72).

Boxer's problem is lack of intelligence, shown in his inability to learn the alphabet. However, it also highlights his tremendous determination, even on retirement when he intended "to devote the rest of his life to learning the remaining twenty-two letters of the alphabet" (p.103). The essential nobility of his character is reflected also in his ambition "to study and improve his mind" (p.103) in retirement. However, Boxer does not have much to improve! An intelligent approach to problems is to analyse and try to find the cause, and hence solutions. Boxer's answer is too simplistic — "I will work harder." This is fine in helping, for example, to provide more food, but it does not get to the *cause* of hunger — that the food is divided up by the pigs in unfair amounts.

Boxer is "as strong as any two ordinary horses put together" (p.6) and this is not used for his own benefit, but in the service of others, and is an inspiration to them: "Boxer was the admiration of everybody ... There were days when the entire work of the farm seemed to rest upon his mighty shoulders" (p.26). This is taken to the level of self-sacrifice and pain, as he gets up earlier than anyone else to go to work, and even works by moonlight, despite pain and old age. "Boxer refused to take even a day off work, and made it a point of honour not to let it be seen that he was in pain" (p.94). It is tragic that someone who gives so much of himself should not be given back the simple reward of a quiet retirement. It is significant that his ambitions are not for himself, but for others: "He had, he said, only one real ambition left — to see the windmill well under way before he reached the age for retirement" (p.94).

Boxer is very useful to the pigs, but because he finally speaks his mind (pp.70-71), and because he is so well-respected by the others, they are prepared to kill him. This is probably because he crossed Squealer in defending Snowball, and Napoleon decided that to disgrace Snowball was more important than Boxer's tremendous productivity and loyalty. Ironically, Boxer had already conceded that if Napoleon said that Snowball was a traitor, it must be right. In a just and fair system, virtue is rewarded, but since the tyranny set up by the pigs is completely exploitative and unfair, Boxer is killed off, to save the expense of looking after him in retirement and ill-health. This is doubly ironic when Squealer talks about "the admirable care he had received, and the expensive medicines for which Napoleon had paid without a thought as to the cost" (p.106).

Most of us believe that sacrifice in a good cause is worthwhile. It is unfortunate that Boxer, who even threw his useful straw hat on the fire (p.20), put his mighty efforts into a cause that was totally corrupt.

Key Points

1. Noble
2. Self-sacrificing
3. Morally brave
4. Physically brave
5. Stupid
6. Extremely strong
7. Well-loved
8. Misplaced loyalty
9. Pathos of his end

Key Quotes

1. "Made it a point of honour not to let it be seen that he was in pain" (p.94).
2. "Boxer would even come out at night and work for an hour or two on his own by the light of the harvest moon" (p.61).
3. "I do not believe that. Snowball fought bravely at the Battle of the Cowshed" (p.70).
4. "Animal Hero, First Class" (p.40).
5. "Boxer could not get beyond the letter D" (p.30).
6. "Nothing could be achieved without Boxer, whose strength seemed equal to that of all the rest of the animals put together" (p.54).
7. "Boxer was the admiration of everybody" (p.26).
8. "Napoleon is always right" (pp.50-51).
9. "The time had been when a few kicks from Boxer's hoofs would have smashed the van to matchwood. But alas! His strength had left him" (pp.104-105).

Benjamin

"Benjamin was the oldest animal on the farm, and the worst tempered. He seldom talked, and when he did it was usually to make some cynical remark — for instance, he would say that God had given him a tail to keep the flies off, but that he would sooner have no tail and no flies. Alone among the animals on the farm he never laughed. If asked why, he would say that he saw nothing to laugh at. Nevertheless, without openly admitting it, he was devoted to Boxer" (p.6).

Benjamin seems to be bitter and bad-tempered. Maybe he is so intelligent that he gets frustrated with the stupidity of others; or maybe in his long life, he has been too often disappointed. However, he does have his good points, like the concern and regard he holds for Boxer, and his bravery in the battles. Although intelligent enough to lead the animals, or at least warn them about what he knows, he chooses not to do so.

For instance, he will not express an opinion about the rebellion. "When asked whether he was not happier now that Jones was gone, he would say only 'Donkeys live a long time. None of you has ever seen a dead donkey,' and the others had to be content with this cryptic answer" (p.27). He is probably saying that he does not trust anyone, or have any hope in a new system; the only way to survive is to avoid trouble. This is a rather cynical, negative view.

His intelligence is outstanding. "Benjamin could read as well as any pig, but never exercised his faculty" (p.30). He is the first to realise that the windmill is to be blown up. On another occasion, Boxer can see that Squealer has fallen off the ladder because he is drunk, but only Benjamin is aware of the full situation — that Squealer was changing the commandment forbidding alcohol. "Benjamin ...

nodded his muzzle with a knowing air, and seemed to understand, but would say nothing" (p.93). Finally, it is Benjamin who discovers that Boxer is being sent to the knackers, even though the pigs try to remove Boxer while the animals are at work. His love for Boxer finally goads him into action. "It was the first time that they had ever seen Benjamin excited — indeed it was the first time that anyone had seen him gallop" (p.103). His rather intolerant, superior attitude is shown when he calls the animals "Fools" because they do not grasp the significance of what is going on until he tells them.

Benjamin shows his bravery in the battles ("Benjamin turned round and lashed at them with his small hoofs", p.37), and he is loved by Boxer — "Perhaps, as Benjamin is growing old too, they will let him retire at the same time and be a companion to me" (p.101) — but it seems a pity that the one animal who is as intelligent as the pigs does not use his intelligence consistently to help the rest of the downtrodden class of animals to which he belongs. He is so cynical and pessimistic that he does not believe that any improvement is possible. "He refused to believe either that the food would become more plentiful or that the wind-mill would save work. Windmill or no windmill, he said, life would go on as it had always gone on — that is, badly" (p.46).

Benjamin represents the disillusioned intelligentsia who realise that revolutions are empty dreams, that, human nature being what it is, power corrupts, and an exploitative ruling class always emerges. George Orwell himself was so pessimistic that his friends called him "Donkey George".

Key Points

1. Intelligent
2. Pessimistic

3. Cynical
4. Passive — refusing to act
5. Brave
6. Superior
7. Uncommunicative
8. Good-hearted

Key Quotes

1. "Benjamin could read as well as any pig, but never exercised his faculty. So far as he knew, he said, there was nothing worth reading" (p.30).

2. "Windmill or no windmill, he said, life would go on as it had always gone on — that is, badly" (p.46).

3. " ... he would say only 'Donkeys live a long time. None of you has ever seen a dead donkey,' and the others had to be content with this cryptic answer" (pp.27-28).

4. "He did his work in the same slow obstinate way as he had done it in Jones's time, never shirking, and never volunteering for extra work either" (p.27).

5. "Benjamin turned round and lashed at them with his small hoofs" (p.37).

6. "Fools! Do you not see what is written on the side of that van?" (p.103).

7. "About the rebellion and its results he would express no opinion" (p.27).

8. (a) "Benjamin urged Boxer to work less hard" (p.94).
   (b) "Benjamin ... lay down at Boxer's side, and, without speaking, kept the flies off him with his long tail" (p.102).

Clover

"A stout motherly mare approaching middle life, who had never quite got her figure back after her fourth foal" (p.6), Clover is Boxer's companion. She is as protective and as caring as he is, displaying a true maternal instinct for the weaker animals. "Clover made a sort of wall round them with her great foreleg, and the ducklings nestled down inside it, and promptly fell asleep" (p.7).

Clover is only a little more intelligent than Boxer (she knows *all* the letters of the alphabet). But it is she who makes the connection between "Four legs good, two legs better" and the breaking of the Seven Commandments (p.114). Even so, she cannot be angry, and her character is revealed as undemonstrative and gentle. "Without saying anything, she tugged gently at his mane and led him round to the end of the big barn, where the Seven Commandments were written" (P114). However, she is very active in trying to save Boxer from being taken away in the knacker's van — "Clover forced her way to the front" (p.104). She is one of the more sensitive of the animals and, although she is unable to express herself very well in words, it is through her that Orwell expresses the bewildered disillusionment of all the animals after the mass confessions and executions (p.74). Clover is presented as a focal point of the animals, as they all are comforted by her motherly nature. "The animals huddled around Clover, not speaking" (p.75). She is thinking "this was not what they had aimed at when they had set themselves years ago to work for the overthrow of the human race" (p.75). She has a very positive, almost idealistic vision of how they should live: "A society of animals set free from hunger and the whip, all equal, each working according to his capacity, the strong protecting the weak" (p.76). Although she herself and Boxer are fine examples of the strong protecting the weak, the unfortunate fact is that on Animal Farm the strong (the pigs in intellect, and the dogs in strength) exploit the weak (the other animals).

The sad thing is that she, and the other animals, are not clever enough to analyse their situation. Despite all the evidence before her eyes, "There was no thought of re-bellion or disobedience in her mind ... Whatever happened she would remain faithful, work hard, carry out the orders that were given to her, and accept the leadership of Napoleon" (p.76). She is unable to see that Napoleon has corrupted the ideals of the revolution, and the animals are already feeling "hunger and the whip". However, she does realise intuitively that something is wrong in the way the commandments are gradually adjusted ("Curiously enough, Clover had not remembered that the Fourth Commandment mentioned sheets; but as it was there on the wall, it must have done so", p.60). She feels disillusioned, and the only way she can express it is in a particularly plaintive singing of "Beasts of England", which helps to comfort the other animals. Ironically, even this small comfort is immediately snatched from them as the song is abolished.

Like Boxer and many others, Clover is never rewarded for her efforts and loyalty ("Boxer and Clover always carried between them a green banner marked with the hoof and the horn and the caption "Long Live Comrade Napoleon!", p.98). She is betrayed by the system that she so willingly supports.

Key Points

1. Maternal
2. Gentle

3. Idealistic
4. Blindly loyal
5. Not intelligent, gullible
6. Sad and disillusioned

Key Quotes

1. "The animals huddled around Clover, not speaking" (p.75).
2. "Clover made a sort of wall round them with her great foreleg, and the ducklings nestled down inside it" (p.7).
3. "Whatever happened she would remain faithful, work hard, carry out the orders that were given to her, and accept the leadership of Napoleon" (p.76).
4. "Clover learnt the whole alphabet, but could not put words together" (p.30).
5. "It was not for this that they had built the windmill and faced the bullets of Jones's guns" (p.76).
6. (Boxer and Clover). "These two had great difficulty in thinking anything out for themselves, but having once accepted the pigs as their teachers, they absorbed everything that they were told, and passed it on to the other animals by simple arguments" (p.17).

Moses

Moses is "Mr Jones's especial pet, ... a spy and a tale-bearer" (p.17). He is occasionally fed by Jones (p.18) and has the additional privilege of sleeping in the farmhouse. This separates him from the other animals. As his name suggests, Moses represents religion, and the part it plays (or does not play) in a revolution. Orwell suggests that organised religion is conservative and traditionalistic, interested in preserving its own security rather than in social justice, and therefore a supporter of the ruling party.

Moses is the only animal not present at Major's speech (p.7). Not only does Moses not attend the meeting, his own philosophy is against rebellion, for he preaches acceptance of suffering now for reward later. He is "a clever talker" and he tells the animals that there is a place called Sugarcandy Mountain to which they go when they die. "In Sugarcandy Mountain it was Sunday seven days a week, clover was in season all the year round, and lump sugar and linseed cake grew on the hedges" (p.17).

Although the animals hate Moses for telling tales and not working, some of them believe in Sugarcandy Mountain. The pigs do not, and in the early days of the rebellion, they try to convince the others.

Significantly, Moses does not stay after the rebellion, but follows Mrs Jones as she flees. He stays away for several years, and then returns with his usual message of Sugarcandy Mountain, which is attractive to some animals: "Their lives now, they reasoned, were hungry and laborious; was it not right and just that a better world should exist somewhere else?" (p.100). The pigs are contemptuous of this simple-minded reasoning, but find it useful in keeping the animals contented, and so "they allowed him to remain on the farm, not working, with an allowance of a gill of beer a day" (p.100).

(The political significance is that in 1944, Stalin was eager to have the sympathy of Roman Catholics, because he anticipated resistance in Poland — a Catholic country — and thought he would become popular by writing a conciliatory letter to the Pope. In general, however, communists see religion as a means of suppression and exploitation — "Religion is the opium of the masses," said Karl Marx, originator of communist thinking. The Russian Orthodox Church always preached loyalty to the Tsar.)

Key Points

1. Dependent on ruling class, whether Jones or the pigs
2. A clever talker
3. Hated and yet believed by some
4. A spy and a tale-bearer

Key Quotes

1. "A thing that was difficult to determine was the attitude of the pigs towards Moses. They all declared contemptuously that his stories about Sugarcandy Mountain were lies, and yet they allowed him to remain on the farm, not working, with an allowance of a gill of beer a day" (p.100).
2. "Sugarcandy Mountain, that happy country where we poor animals shall rest for ever from our labours!" (p.99).
3. "The animals hated Moses because he told tales and did not work" (p.17).
4. "Moses, who was Mr Jones's especial pet, was a spy and a tale-bearer" (p.17).

Mollie

Mollie is stupid, vain, and only interested in attention and comfort. She "began flirting her white mane, hoping to draw attention to the red ribbons it was plaited with" (p.7). In the farmhouse, she is scolded for "admiring herself in the glass in a very foolish manner" (p.22). She is also lazy and evasive: "Mollie ... was not good at getting up in the morning, and had a way of leaving work early on the grounds that there was a stone in her hoof" (p.27). She is not very clever, but even so, is so vain that she "refused to learn any but the six letters which spelt her own name" (p.30).

Mollie is also a coward. After the Battle of the Cowshed, she was found "hiding in her stall with her head buried among the hay in the manger" (p.39). Her behaviour becomes very unsatisfactory and suspicious: "On every kind of pretext she would run away from work and go to the drinking pool, where she would stand foolishly gazing at her own reflection in the water" (p.41). Even though luxuries and frivolities are forbidden, Clover discovers that Mollie has hidden for herself ribbons and lump sugar. Later, she runs away and appears to be enjoying herself working for a man of doubtful character. She debases herself for the sake of comfort and pleasure.

Mollie represents those who do not care about anything except themselves. Utterly self-indulgent, they are too vain, self-centred and selfish to consider the good of all, or the need for principle or self-sacrifice. Their outlook is just immediate personal pleasure, not long-term gain for everyone.

The Cat

The cat is more lazy and evasive than Mollie, but presented in a humorous way, as her behaviour is entirely unpredictable. In the first vote, for instance, "The cat ... was afterwards discovered to have voted on both sides" (p.11). This is because she has not listened to Major's speech, being more interested, as usual, in her own comfort: "The cat ... looked around, as usual, for the warmest place" (p.7).

She is very lazy: "When there was work to be done, the cat could never be found. She would vanish for hours on end, and then reappear at meal-times, or in the evening after work was over" (p.27). However, she has a charming manner, and manages to get away with it: "But she always made such excellent excuses, and purred so affectionately, that it was impossible not to believe in her good intentions" (p.27).

Amusingly, she serves diligently for a while on Snowball's Re-education Committee, in order to try to catch the sparrows! She told them that "all animals were now comrades and that any sparrow who chose could come and perch on her paw; but the sparrows kept their distance" (p.29). It is significant that this lazy cat was very active on the Committee "for some days" only. Without sparrows to eat, she is not interested any more!

She is always ready to take food, but avoids responsibility and has a fine sense of self-preservation. The cat is the only animal not present when the mass confessions and executions take place: "The cat ... had suddenly disappeared just before Napoleon ordered the animals to assemble" (p.74).

Nevertheless, she does not totally lack courage: "Even the cat suddenly leapt off a roof on to a cowman's shoulders and sank her claws in his neck" (p.38). The use of the word "Even" in "even the cat" indicates that because the cat is uncooperative and selfish, she is the animal least expected to fight, but she does.

The Other Animals

The dogs, Bluebell and Jessie are the mothers of the nine puppies who eventually became Napoleon's ferocious enforcement squad. They and the other dog, **Pincher,** are quite mild compared to their offspring, but a hint of their aggressive tendencies is to be seen when they (and the cat) are the only ones to vote against rats being treated as comrades.

Muriel, the white goat, is quite intelligent. She can read well and she "sometimes used to read to the others in the evenings from scraps of newspaper which she found on the rubbish heap" (p.30). These scraps of information are valued by Muriel, who uses her talent for the benefit of others — one of the few who do.

The other animals are all referred to as groups, not individuals: the hens, the sheep, the rats and wild animals, the young porkers (pigs), the pigeons.

The hens, led by three young Black Minorca pullets, "made a determined effort to thwart Napoleon's wishes" (p.66) when they rebel against Napoleon's decision to sell their eggs, but they are ruthlessly starved into surrender. They represent the down-trodden masses.

The sheep, like the hens, cannot read, but are very fond of repetition: "the sheep developed a great liking for this maxim, and often as they lay in the field they would all start bleating 'Four legs good, two legs bad! Four legs good, two legs bad!' and keep it up for hours on end, never growing tired of it" (p.31). Sheep are traditionally stupid creatures, incapable of independent thought and action, and so are easily manipulated by the pigs. Napoleon trains them to vote for him as a block, and to interrupt Snowball's speeches, or any other attempt at democratic discussion, by loud, non-stop chanting of the slogan, "Four legs good, two legs better". They are gullible and unthinking, representing those people who talk in cliches or stock phrases heard elsewhere. This lack of intelligence is shown when they are taught (even though it takes a week!) "Four legs good, two legs better". Ironically, they enthusiastically aid their own slavery!

The rats are the outsiders of society, not domesticated and productive like the other animals. They are classed with the wild animals (such as rabbits) and perhaps they are associated with the outsiders such as criminals, gypsies and tribal minorities in Russia (Russia was — and is — a vast federation of different ethnic and language groups). Major recognises the problem at the beginning: "The wild creatures, such as rats and rabbits — are they our friends or enemies? Let us put it to the vote. I propose this question to the meeting: Are rats comrades?" (p.11). They are overwhelmingly accepted by the animals, except for their natural enemies, the cat and the dogs. (Perhaps the dogs represent that narrow-minded section of society which is intolerant of any who do not conform.) The rats are never held in high esteem, not even by kind-hearted Clover. When she reflects on the horror of the mass executions, she says, "Since Jones had left the farm, until today, no animal had killed another animal. Not even a rat had been killed" (p.74).

The young porkers are intelligent, articulate and have a social conscience, but are intimidated and eventually executed after forced confessions. When Napoleon announces that the meetings are to be abolished, "Four young porkers in the front row uttered shrill squeals of disapproval, and all four sprang to their feet and began speaking at once" (p.49). But they are silenced by the dogs. Later, when Napoleon breaks more of the resolutions agreed on by the animals (e.g. not to have any dealings with human beings) "the four young pigs who had protested when Napoleon abolished the Meetings raised their voices timidly, but they were promptly silenced by a tremendous growling from the dogs" (p.57). Why they finally confess in such detail to being in league with Snowball is not stated, but presumably they were tortured, threatened or forced. The fact that they are immediately executed indicates both Napoleon's fear and ruthlessness.

The parallel in Stalin's day was the trial of Zinoviev and Kamenev (who formed a ruling triumvirate with Stalin in 1923) in 1939 who confessed to fantastic charges of radicalism. Why? "Although several factors contributed to bringing the men to the point of making these confessions, they made them at the last in the sincere conviction that this was their sole remaining service to the Party and the Revolution. They sacrificed honour as well as life to defend the hated regime of Stalin, because it contained the last faint gleam of hope for that better world to which they had consecrated themselves in early youth" (W. G. Krivitsky, *I Was Stalin's Agent* — H. Hamilton, 1939).

The young porkers who speak up illustrate the fact that not all of the pigs (or any one class or section of society) are without conscience. They stand to gain from Napoleon's policies, but they speak up to defend points of principle.

The other "confessions" by other animals are progressively more ridiculous and laughable, and this illustrates part of Orwell's satirical technique. He believes that it is better to mock stupidity and lies than adopt a high moral tone which bores the reader.

The Humans

The human beings in this book are caricatures or types, and are obvious symbols of the political set-up. Jones represents the old ruling class, which is now decadent and worn out, and, in the context of Russia, the Tsar, who ruled his subjects in a cruel, feudal manner. Frederick represents Fascism, the cruel one-party rule of such as Adolf Hitler. Pilkington symbolises Capitalism. He is lazy, uncaring, greedy and exploitative of the working classes. Whymper is one of those opportunists who take advantage of any situation, and often are made unsuspecting dupes.

Jones represents all that is evil in the master/worker relationship. As old Major explains to them: "Man is the only real enemy we have. Remove Man from the scene, and the root cause of hunger and overwork is abolished for ever" (p.9). Not only that, but Jones is cruel: "Every one of you will scream your lives out at the block within a year. To that horror we all must come — cows, pigs, hens, sheep, everyone" (p.10).

Jones is a drunk whose laziness brings about his own downfall. "Mr Jones, although a hard master, had been a capable farmer, but of late he had fallen on evil days" (p.18). He drinks to console himself, neglects to feed the animals, and is driven out in a spontaneous rebellion.

Other references to Jones in the book deal with his unsuccessful attempt to retake the farm (a counter-revolution); his exile in the Red Lion (many of the Russian ruling class fled to Paris where they led comfortable lives); and his death is an "inebriates' home" (p.108). However, his name is still important, as it is exploited by the pigs to frighten the animals into accepting any hardship or any lies: "Surely none of you wishes to see Jones back? The animals reassured him on this point immediately" (p.60). All the evil that is heaped onto Snowball is also associated with Jones: "He was Jones's secret agent all the time" (p.69).

Frederick represents Hitler and Pinchfield, Germany. His name is possibly reminiscent of Frederick The Great of Prussia, and Pinchfield suggests the iron discipline and efficiency that Hitler imposed on Germany during his rule

(1933-1945). Frederick is "a tough, shrewd man, perpetually involved in lawsuits and with a name for driving hard bargains" (p.35). He is portrayed as very devious (sly and cunning) and also very cruel. He double-crosses Napoleon over the timber, and then, far from being a friend, attacks Animal Farm and destroys the windmill. However, this only infuriates the animals into an all-out and successful counter-attack. (A parallel event marred relations between Germany and Russia — Russia supplied Germany with a lot of oil in 1938-9 and signed a non-aggression pact in 1939. Germany invaded and devastated much of Russia's industry in 1941-2, but was eventually defeated.) Frederick's legendary cruelty — "he had killed a dog by throwing it into a furnace" (p.82) — is an allusion to the Jews being incinerated in millions on Hitler's orders.

Pilkington of Foxwood represents the capitalists who have accumulated vast riches (perhaps through colonisation) and now have no incentive to improve. They merely want to maintain the *status quo* (keep things as they are), and this leads to laziness and neglect. Foxwood is "a large, neglected old-fashioned farm" (p.34), and Mr Pilkington, "an easy-going gentleman farmer who spent most of his time in fishing or hunting" (p.34). Together, they represent the British Empire in decline.

Frederick and Pilkington "disliked each other so much that it was difficult for them to come to any agreement, even in defence of their own interests" (p.35). They also scorn the idea of animals managing a farm for themselves and spread pernicious rumours about Animal Farm.

When the pigs, as a ruling class, become friendly with the farmers as a ruling class, Pilkington speaks on their behalf. He is impressed by the fact that "the lower animals on Animal Farm did more work and received less food than any animals in the county" (p.117). The fact that the pigs have more in common with Pilkington and the farmers is reflected in Pilkington's attempt at witticism: "If you have your lower animals to contend with, he said, we have our lower classes!" (p.118). Former enemies have become friends because they wish to maintain their position of advantage over the classes they exploit. However bad Pilkington is, he is a little better than the Hitler-like Frederick: "The animals distrusted Pilkington, as a human being, but greatly preferred him to Frederick, whom they both feared and hated" (p.82).

Whymper, as his name suggests, is an unattractive person. Self-seeking and unprincipled, he only wants to make money out of Animal Farm: "A sly-looking little man ... sharp enough to have realized earlier than anyone else that Animal Farm would need a broker and that the commissions would be worth having" (p.58). He is also stupid, and is duped into spreading the news that Animal Farm has food when, in fact, the animals are starving: "He was deceived and continued to report to the outside world that there was no food shortage on Animal Farm" (p.66).

In general, the humans are hostile to Animal Farm, and yet gradually have to recognise its achievements. "The human beings did not hate Animal Farm any less now that it was prospering; indeed, they hated it more than ever ... And yet, against their will, they had developed a certain respect for the efficiency with which the animals were managing their own affairs" (p.58).

INTERPRETATION

What is *Animal Farm* about? Apart from telling a good story, a book like this carries a message. (In fact, one of the major criticisms of *Animal Farm* is that it is too "didactic", that is, that the message is too obvious and heavy.) Although young people can enjoy it as a charming fairy tale, it makes some very serious points, not about animals, but about human nature in general, and politics in particular. So the book can be understood on three levels:

(1) The fairy-story level, where the simplicity of language, the clear story line, the triumphs and disasters, the noble characters and the villains, can be easily understood (and enjoyed) by young children.

(2) The "human nature in general" level. Although the characters are rather two-dimensional, they are sufficiently rounded, and presented in sufficient variety, to examine the idea that Power corrupts, and that goodness, determination, and self-sacrifice can be exploited by the selfish and the ruthless. An examination of human motivation and personality types is a rewarding study, although the characters in *Animal Farm* are not perhaps as psychologically complex as Jane Eyre or Lady Macbeth.

(3) As political satire. How much need a sixteen-year-old Singaporean know about Russian history and politics to appreciate this novel? There is no doubt that Orwell wrote this book as a political satire, and therefore one needs to know the background to appreciate fully the author's intention. It is important to realise that much of it *is* background, and to appreciate the fact that Orwell could not have brought his views of recent

modern history to the attention of millions of people by writing a history book. Satire is a literary technique which uses wit, irony and humour to ridicule vice or folly. In *Animal Farm* Orwell succeeds in exposing the brutality of Stalin/Napoleon in particular, and the idea that "power tends to corrupt and absolute power corrupts absolutely".

This saying (by Lord Acton) means that anyone given power/responsibility has a natural tendency to use it for his own self-interest. If you have only a limited amount of power, other people can check your abuses, because it might go against *their* self-interest, or the general good. But if you have "absolute power", no one can check you or stop you, so that concern for others, or the general good, is ignored as you pursue more and more selfish aims, ultimately causing misery for anyone who gets in your way. Friends, family, religion, ideals, beliefs are all abandoned because there is no restraint. "Corrupt" means to make bad or evil, to lose all normal human decency and consideration for what is right and wrong.

Animal Farm is not only a satire on how the high ideals of the Russian Revolution (equality, freedom and prosperity) are crushed by Stalin's ruthless brutality, but a comment on how *all* tyrannies (a tyranny is a brutal enforcement of authority which will not tolerate any opposition) are evil. Mr Pilkington represents Capitalism (where the owners, motivated by profit, exploit their workers), especially that of Britain, but the other Western powers also. Frederick represents Hitler and his brand of Fascism (belief that the party and the state are above the individual; stresses absolute obedience to a glorified leader). So Orwell is criticising, not just Stalin's Russia, but the Capitalist system of Britain,

America and the West in general; also the repressive Nazi regime in Germany. What he is saying is that all three are tyrannies. The initial spark of a revolution, the original intention of a constitution may have been an ideal of the good life, but the result is always the same — tyranny. Communism is no more or less evil than Fascism or Capitalism — they are all used by the pigs as a means of satisfying their greed and lust for power. According to Orwell, religion is used by the oppressors as a device to divert the minds of the sufferers. Moses the raven, who is always talking about the sweet, eternal life of Sugarcandy Mountain, flees with Jones, but returns when Napoleon has established his own tyranny.

Socialism

Although born into a privileged class, George Orwell was a socialist, believing in a more equal distribution of property and wealth, and public ownership of industry, banking and transport.

Written in 1943-4, towards the end of World War II in which Britain and Russia were allies fighting against Germany, *Animal Farm* was intended to counter the widespread view that Socialism = Stalinism. Russia, as a war ally, was very popular in England, and Orwell was trying to prepare readers against disillusionment with socialism when Stalin's excesses became known. He said, "Russian behaviour is not worse than that of Capitalist governments. The point is the effect of the Russian myth on the socialist movement *here* (i.e. in England). Nothing has contributed so much to the corruption of the original idea of Socialism as the belief that Russia is a Socialist country." Orwell attacks Stalinism and shows that Socialism is a welcome change from oppression (even though it is vulnerable to betrayal).

However, most readers still think (mistakenly) that Orwell is criticising Socialism. Socialism does exist, in near ideal form, in Chapters Three and Four. "The animals were happy as they never conceived it possible to be. Every mouthful of food was an acute positive pleasure, now that it was truly their own food, produced by themselves and for themselves, not doled out to them by a grudging master" (p.26). They have leisure, free speech, democracy and education. However, the unfair monopoly of the milk and apples by the pigs is an indication of future abuse.

Of course, Soviet critics deny any particular criticism of Russia or of Communism. They claim that *Animal Farm* is critical only of bureaucracy (excessively centralised government, controlling every aspect of life, and very inefficient because of its "red tape").

T. S. Eliot, the great poet, was also a publisher who refused to publish *Animal Farm*. He admitted that the story was "a distinguished piece of writing", but argued that "the effect is simply one of negation. The book ought to excite sympathy with what the author wants, as well as with his objectives." He felt that Orwell's "generally Trotskyite" point of view was not convincing.

William Empson agreed. He said, "Your (i.e. Orwell's) point of view of course is that the animals ought to have gone on sharing Animal Farm. But your metaphor — the intellectual superiority of the pigs — suggests that the Russian Revolution was a pathetically impossible effort to defy nature. You must expect to be 'misunderstood' about this book on a large scale." So the final irony — especially as the story is written in such crystal-clear, simple style — is that *Animal Farm* is often misunderstood. Orwell's message does not get through.

Utopia

A Utopia is a perfect world. The word is derived from the name of a book by Sir Thomas More (English statesman and martyr). The idea is not new. The ancient Greek philosopher, Plato, discussed an ideal world in his *Republic*. Jonathan Swift, in *Gulliver's Travels,* took a satirical look at such worlds, and discovered the flaws in such thinking. The term "Shangri-la" means a place of eternal youth and peace.

In *Animal Farm*, Major gives the animals a vision of such perfection, which is enshrined in the revolutionary song "Beasts of England" (a reference to "The Internationale", the song of the International Labour movement). This theme is taken up by Snowball, with his promise of a three-day week and luxurious living standards, and bleakly remembered by Clover in its essentials: "If she herself had had any picture of the future, it had been of a society of animals set free from hunger and the whip, all equal, each working according to his capacity, the strong protecting the weak" (p.75).

This idealistic vision of a Utopia is balanced by other views — of Moses, with his "lies" of "Sugarcandy Mountain"; of Napoleon, with his own private Utopia of unlimited power and self-glory; and, to a lesser extent, the negative Utopia of the capitalist Pilkington, who admires "the low rations, the long working hours, and the general absence of pampering ... on Animal Farm" (p.118).

THEMES

Themes are the ideas which reoccur and are explored through the book. Apart from the ideas discussed in the Interpretation Section, there are as many "themes" as there are points of view about the book: what is important to one reader does not strike another at all. Consider these few and then find your own "message":

1. Power — tyranny
2. Corruption
3. Utopia
4. Bureaucracy
5. Self-sacrifice
6. Exploitation
7. Propaganda
8. Gullibility
9. Hypocrisy
10. Education.

Some of these have already been dealt with, but some others need a little explanation.

Bureaucracy

A bureaucracy is a highly centralised form of administration in which officials control every detail of public and private life, subject only to their superior officers and without any responsibility for their acts to the people. We have all experienced bureaucracy in making complaints to a large organisation, or often when travelling abroad. One can never get to the person who is actually making decisions, and the inquiry/complaint is passed on, and on, and on. Very often it relies on "red-tape" i.e. endless rules, regulations, form-filling. It lacks the personal touch most of us need in seeking decisions affecting our lives. Otherwise we feel helpless, lost in a vast, uncaring, impersonal machine.

In Singapore, for instance, the Government has set up Town Councils to give people a say in their local affairs, and actually take part in them. The police have set up small, neighbourhood posts for better communications and a personal, friendly touch. Most hotels, banks and other large institutions stress service to the customer as an individual, with a friendly, personal touch. All this is aimed at keeping people happy, treating them as human beings with feelings and needs, rather than as economic units. In this way, the faults of a bureaucracy are avoided.

In *Animal Farm,* the rebellion starts with high democratic ideals (even the rats are accepted as comrades) and all the animals are involved in decision-making at the weekly meetings. However, even in the early days, the pigs take the lead in putting forward resolutions (suggestions to be voted on) and "other animals understood how to vote, but could never think of any resolutions of their own" (p.28). This is one of the reasons for a bureaucracy to take shape — people opting out of their right to participate. Later, it goes a stage further. "It had come to be accepted that the pigs, who were manifestly cleverer than the other animals, should decide all questions of farm policy, though their decisions had to be ratified by a majority vote" (p.42). Already, control is being given up, leading to the struggle for power between Snowball and Napoleon. When Napoleon drives out Snowball by force, Napoleon abolishes the meetings, and announces that "all questions relating to the working of the farm would be settled by a special committee of pigs, presided over by himself. These would meet in private and afterwards communicate their decisions to the others" (p.49). Squealer explains Napoleon's thinking: "He would be only too happy to let you make your decisions for yourselves. But sometimes you might make the wrong

decisions, comrades, and then where should we be?" (p.50)
The animals try to speak up, but are no match for Squealer.
They are being stripped of their rights, and actually trust
Napoleon's judgement and incorruptibility.

The way in which Napoleon announces these changes is
significant. He mounts the platform previously used by
Major. He is putting himself as leader above the rest, and
taking this role (which was Major's by virtue of wisdom and
general approval) without consultation.

Now, the animals only meet for ceremonial activities, and
to receive orders. They take no part in the decision-making
process. "They did not sit all together as they had done in
the past" (p.51) — the pigs and dogs sat on a raised platform facing the rest. From now on, decisions are announced
without any explanations (e.g. the decision to build the
windmill) and decisions affecting the working conditions
of the animals (increased hours, work on Sundays, reduced
rations, no retirement scheme) and the general principles
of Animalism (no trade with humans, no human vices, the
re-writing of the Seven Commandments) are now issued by
decree, that is, at Napoleon's personal decision, without
consulting even the other pigs. The decisions are enforced
by the dogs, and Squealer "explains", to ease the worries
of the animals. Despite their misgivings, there is now no
way to express their views, they are so remote from the
centre of power. Napoleon becomes increasingly distant
from the ordinary animals, and even from the other pigs.
"Napoleon inhabited separate apartments from the others.
He took his meals alone" (p.79). Also, Napoleon no longer
gives the orders in person. "All orders were now issued
through Squealer or one of the other pigs. Napoleon himself
was not seen in public as often as once a fortnight" (p.79).
With the cult of personality making Napoleon seem in-

capable of error, and always acting in the best interests of the animals, the process of bureaucracy, executed by the pigs and enforced by the dogs, is complete.

Propaganda

Originally this term meant "spreading of the faith" but it has now come to mean the systematic spread of only one view by:

(1) suppressing free speech and eliminating opposition;
(2) distorting news by selection (not telling *all* of the facts), suppression (not telling *any* of the facts), or downright lies;
(3) organising campaigns based on statistics, slogans, songs, speeches; holding mass rallies with entertainment value; generally relying on a simplified message and emotional appeal.

Goebbels, Paul Joseph, was Hitler's Minister of Propaganda (1933-45) whose principle was "The bigger the lie, the more it is believed." In *Animal Farm*, Squealer is the Minister of Propaganda, and his job is to distract the animals, and the outside world, from the truth. Whatever Napoleon does (it is usually against the commandments and the animals' interests), Squealer's job is to explain it away. His master gives the first example of propaganda tactics: "What is going to happen to all that milk? said someone ... Never mind the milk, comrades! ... The harvest is more important" (p.24). An important question is brushed aside by focusing on the excitement of the harvest. Already, the principle of equality and fair play has gone.

Point one, suppressing free speech and eliminating opposition, is the work of Napoleon and the dogs. Propaganda (Squealer's job) cannot survive in a democracy, because courageous and intelligent people will ask awkward questions. Even someone like Boxer is attacked because he dared to remember the truth about Snowball. The four young porkers have their throats torn out because they had dared to speak up for democracy (when Napoleon abolished the meetings). In an atmosphere of terror, where no one dare speak, it is easy to put across a single, unified point of view. It is also easy to make a basic misjudgement, such as when Boxer declares "Napoleon is always right".

Propaganda is the advertising side of politics. In advertising, you sell a product by stressing its good points, its superiority over other similar products. Sometimes, less scrupulous advertisers try to sell by denigrating competitive products. In politics, the aim is to stay in power, and to achieve this, some politicians resort to character assassination. This is what happens to Snowball. Immediately after his expulsion, Squealer brands him a "criminal", even though, at this stage, Snowball's bravery and heroism in the Battle of the Cowshed cannot be denied. But by stages, Snowball becomes "Blackball", a hero becomes villain. Squealer has such a talent for re-writing and fabricating history that the animals are almost convinced: "Now when Squealer described the scene so graphically, it seemed to the animals that they did remember it. At any rate, they remembered that at the critical moment of the battle Snowball had turned to flee" (p.71). Squealer has *selected* one fact — that Snowball did turn and appear to flee (but this was a tactic to trap the humans) — and *distorted* it into treachery. So often, so systematically, Snowball is smeared and associated with every trouble and misfortune, that the animals are brainwashed even into believing that he milks the cows in their sleep!

Squealer is "very persuasive" and can "turn black into white". After Napoleon's abrupt decisions "Squealer made a round of the farm to set the animals' minds at rest'' (p.57). This is the normal method — first, aggressive assertion, then gentle persuasion, usually by casting doubt on the victims' memory: "Are you certain that this is not something you have dreamed, comrades? Have you any record of such a resolution? Is it written down anywhere?'' (p.57). Squealer is too clever for them, and, in any case, the pigs are the only source of information.

A good example of propaganda, of image-making, is the cover up of the food-shortage on Animal Farm. "It was vitally necessary to conceal this fact from the outside world'' (p.65). Whymper is given the impression that the grain-bins are full, when they actually contain sand, and "selected animals, mostly sheep'', are rehearsed to tell the lie that "rations had been increased''. Likewise, Squealer's statistics try to mask hunger, although the animals "would sooner have had less figures and more food'' (p.79).

Squealer's principle tasks are:

(1) to disgrace Snowball,
(2) to distort the living standards of the animals,
(3) to glorify Napoleon into near-God status, and
(4) to re-write the commandments.

He succeeds in all of this, and the saddest thing of all is that it is achieved because of the passivity of the masses (after a little opposition in the beginning). With the exception of Benjamin, he succeeds in "fooling all of the people, all of the time''.

Education

The importance of education is first highlighted by Major. He educates the animals into political awareness by clear and forceful speech. He teaches them an important and memorable song which is to influence them for years. Significantly, it has been part of a lost tradition "sung by the animals of long ago and... lost to memory for generations" (p.12). Major gives them a sense of identity and confidence, and a vision of a golden future. His song appeals to their memory and imagination, two vital elements in education. It inspires them to seek self-fulfilment and justice.

Later, education becomes very different. "The work of teaching and organizing the others fell naturally upon the pigs, who were generally recognized as being the cleverest of the animals" (p.15). It is moral/theoretical: "the principles of Animalism" (first encapsuled in the Seven Commandments (p.23), then debased to "Four legs good, two legs bad", for the benefit of the stupider animals); and practical: "blacksmithing, carpentering, and other necessary arts from books" (p.29).

The key to it all is the ability to read, which the pigs do "perfectly". The other animals fail lamentably, except for Muriel, who uses her ability to keep the others informed by reading scraps from the newspapers to them. Benjamin wastes his ability, as he chooses not to use it; the dogs are only interested in the rule of law (the Seven Commandments); Mollie is only interested in self, not in self-improvement; and most of the others cannot even get further than the letter A. This makes it easy for the pigs to manipulate them.

Snowball is an intellectual who reads widely; a Renaissance pig! He is political theorist, philosopher, civil engineer, farmer, designer and military strategist. He has read *The Farmer and Stockbreeder, Electricity for Beginners,* and *Julius Caesar.* "The birds did not understand Snowball's long words, but they accepted his explanation" (p.31). This single sentence shows that Snowball combines brain power with charisma (outstanding personal magnetism, ability to convince and inspire others).

Snowball's and Napoleon's attitudes to education are strongly contrasted. Snowball is for the education of *all* the animals (even though his enthusiasm is comical, his schemes so over-ambitious that they are bound to fail). Napoleon sees education as a means to power. He wants education for a select few only. "Napoleon took no interest in Snowball's committees. He said that the education of the young was more important than anything that could be done for those who were already grown up" (p.31). Napoleon's idea of education is to:

(1) train the puppies to be totally obedient and loyal to himself,

(2) to use Squealer (and to a lesser extent, Minimus the poet) to brainwash the animals with slogans, songs, ceremonies and "Spontaneous Demonstrations", and

(3) to perpetuate power by having his own offspring (31 young pigs) specially educated.

A final ironic twist is that the pigs, for all their intelligence, finally subscribe to very poor publications like *John Bull*, Tit-bits and *The Daily Mirror* (very light reading, scorned by the intelligentsia).

LITERARY FEATURES

Humour

The surface humour and the light bantering tone of *Animal Farm* are part of the convention of beast fables. Orwell uses the apparently frivolous form of the animal tale to convey with immense power his profoundly bitter message. These comic moments have a disturbing element of cruelty. While Snowball is organising The Egg Production Committee for the hens, the Clean Tails League for the cows, the Wild Comrades Re-education Committee and the Whiter Wool Movement (one wonders how this could be achieved), Napoleon is carefully educating the dogs for his own evil purposes. Similarly, the "confessions" forced from the animals are very funny. A goose confesses to stealing six ears of corn — a very small amount — and only to eat, not for profit. A sheep urinates in the drinking pool — as if this could have been planned by someone as intelligent as Snowball! Surely he could have thought of some more effective way of poisoning the farm. Chasing an old ram round a bonfire is more like a schoolboy prank, which conjures up a comical image. It is worthy of a mild reproof, not execution. And the influence of Snowball in these "crimes" is ridiculously far-fetched. Yet this humour is sharply contrasted with the viciousness of the dogs tearing out the throats of the "guilty" parties.

There is also a touch of pathos in some of the humour. The silliness of Mollie, admiring herself in the mirror and refusing "to learn any but the six letters" (p.30) of her own name, masks the real unhappiness she feels at being denied the ribbons, sugar and attention of former days. In contrast; Boxer's self-sacrifice in destroying his straw hat is comic but sad, because he needs the hat for practical purposes, but he associates it with slavery. Boxer's attempts to read are also praiseworthy, but comic.

Similarly, the way in which the cat tries to tempt the sparrows on to her paw is funny, as long as one considers it natural to the cat, and not as a depressing example of exploitation and hypocrisy.

Some of the humour is achieved by the unexpected reminders that the animals are actually animals, and not, as we inevitably tend to think of them, humans. "With some difficulty (for it is not easy for a pig to balance himself on a ladder) Snowball climbed up" (p.23). Also, the modern industrial efficiency of production statistics, and Squealer's skill at presenting them, is suddenly highlighted by the fact that Squealer is a pig, dealing with reading, writing, and arithmetic. "Squealer, holding down a long strip of paper with his trotter, would read out to them lists of figures" (p.79).

There is humour too in Napoleon's self-glory, from his titles (Ducklings' Friend) to his pomposity ("he was attended not only by his retinue of dogs but by a black cockerel who marched in front of him and acted as a kind of trumpeter, letting out a loud 'cock-a-doodle-doo' before Napoleon spoke' p.79). The stupidity of the claims made on behalf of Napoleon is also comic. "Under the guidance of our Leader, Comrade Napoleon, I have laid five eggs in six days" (p.80). The poem by Minimus in praise of Napoleon is also bathetic. (Bathos means a descent from the formal and dignified to a ridiculous level, such as "Lord of the swill-bucket". "Lord" is a dignified term, and we would expect Napoleon to be Lord of something important, not the lowly "swill-bucket".) The comparison of a sucking pig to a pint-bottle or rolling pin is also humorous, and the use of low terms like "belly" are comically inappropriate in what is supposed to be a hymn of praise. Mayakovsky, a poet of the revolution who later committed suicide, wrote in "Hymn to J. V. Stalin":

> The world has no person
> Deeper, closer.
> With him, happiness is happier,
> And the sun brighter.

Napoleon is the main target of Orwell's satire, such as when he sends to Pilkington for help. In such a serious situation we usually expect formal language in a proper letter, but all Pilkington sends is "a scrap of paper" and the language of primary school squabbles: "Serves you right" (p.87). Napoleon, for all his mighty power, can be made to look ridiculous — when he is "wounded", it is just the tip of his tail that is "chipped" by a pellet. Nevertheless, he confers on himself the Order of the Green Banner.

The way in which Napoleon suffers from too much alcohol and then turns to brewing his own beer, is also grimly funny, as Squealer relates the details of Napoleon's apparent death-bed wish to ban alcohol, amazing recovery and reversal of the commandment forbidding alcohol. It is not often that Napoleon is outsmarted, but when Frederick cheats him, it is all the funnier because Napoleon has made a public spectacle out of his supposed victory. "Smiling beatifically, and wearing both his decorations, Napoleon reposed on a bed of straw on the platform, with the money at his side" (p.86).

Some of the humour is very light, and some is quite sardonic in tone. Some may feel that there is no humour at all in the way Squealer and Boxer have different views of the Battle of the Windmill. "Then we have won back what we had before," said Boxer. "That is our victory," said Squealer" (p.90). Can we smile at Boxer's bewilderment? Can we marvel at Squealer's barefaced, distorted optimism?

Even so, the light touch is always there to strike a balance. Who cannot chuckle at the completely unexpected, but characteristic action of Napoleon in urinating on Snowball's plans! Who cannot smile at the spelling of "friend" and the handwriting of the 'S' in the commandments!

Beast Fables

The beast fable is an ancient satiric technique in which the characteristic poses of human vice and folly are totally embodied in animals. *Aesop's Fables* are the most famous, such as the one of the fox and the sour grapes. (The French writer, La Fontaine, was influenced by Aesop.)

Children can enjoy and understand the simple moral truths of many fables. The typical fable contains a basic lesson — the good are rewarded and the bad are justly punished — and children readily identify with the lovable animals, rejecting the evil. The tone of such stories is light, slightly mocking and good-humoured. The simplicity of some of the animals in Orwell's story (especially Boxer) is easy to appreciate, such as their child-like joy the day after the rebellion: "suddenly remembering the glorious thing that had happened, they all raced out into the pasture together" (p.20). The key-word is "raced". In the early days of the rebellion, everything was done at break-neck speed, showing tremendous enthusiasm.

However, the message conveyed in a fable need not be light-hearted. The very idea of representing human characteristics in animals is in itself rather pessimistic. Essential to the successful fable is the author's power to keep his reader conscious simultaneously of the human traits satirised and of the animals as animals. The story-teller must never allow the animals to be simply beasts, in which case the piece becomes a non-satirical children's story, or to be merely transparent symbols, in which case the piece becomes a dull sermon. Orwell managed to keep this delicate balance.

THE EXAMINATION

How to Pass

"IF". A small word with a big meaning. If you work through the book thoroughly so that you have a good knowledge of the story, characters, and intentions of the author, you have the basic material to pass, and pass well. If you have this knowledge, it would be a pity to fail because you do not know how to write an answer for the examination. What, therefore, can go wrong?

Each year examiners write reports which detail what was good or bad about the answers given by thousands of candidates world-wide. Each year, certain basic faults are noted, namely:

1. Failure to read the question properly.
2. Failure to focus on key words.
3. Long irrelevant answers.
4. A misguided desire to reproduce everything by heart.
5. Inability to refer to the text properly.

Fault Number One: failure to read the question properly. Many candidates see only one part of the question, and answer that. Take one example: "The best way to read *Animal Farm* is not for the comments and lessons, but for the story and characters." Show how far you agree with this opinion by writing about *three* of your favourite animals as they appear in the novel. Candidates focus on the three animals, give very good accounts of them, and show knowledge of the story, but ignore the "comments and lessons". Even if you totally agree that the best way to read the novel is to focus on story and characters, you must make some judgement on the comments and lessons — you might say that they are distracting, didactic (a frequent criticism of *Animal Farm*, meaning over-stressing the moral of the story) tedious or unnecessary. In saying this, of course, you must give examples; for instance, when Clover reflects on the savagery of the executions and the betrayal of Major's ideals, it is the *author's* reflections, not her own, as shown by the words, "If she could have spoken her thoughts" (p.75).

Fault Number Two: failure to focus on key words. Key words in this example are: "comments and lessons" and "how far" ("three" and "animals" are obviously basic, so if you write about only two animals, or four, *or* about human beings instead of animals, you will be penalised). "Comments and lessons" can be taken as two separate parts. You may note that there are no direct comments, only implied criticism. Because *Animal Farm* is a satire, the "comment" is unnecessary because the faults criticised are obvious, e.g., "from somewhere or other the pigs had acquired the money to buy themselves another case of whisky" (p.107). The comment, or conclusion to be drawn, is that the pigs got the money from the sale of Boxer's body to the glue factory. The "lessons" sometimes come in the form of a direct analysis, by Major, or Benjamin ("Do you not understand what that means? They are taking Boxer to the knacker's!" p.104) but more usually they are implied. In this same episode of Boxer being taken off to the knacker's, the gullibility of the animals is illustrated twice. Once when they believe that Boxer is just going off to hospital, and just say goodbye (p.103), and secondly when they accept Squealer's explanation that the knacker's name had not yet been painted over by the veterinary surgeon. "The animals were enormously relieved to hear this" (p.106). The implied lesson is that you should never take things on face value.

Other examples given by the examiners are: the misreading of phrases like "ideas and activities". Some candidates write only about the chief character's *ideas* and forget to write about his *activities*. "Up to this point in the story" means exactly that, and you will be penalised if you write about what happened after this point in the story. Often a question asks about "a relationship" between two characters, and it is not enough to write two separate character sketches without examining the relationship. Other examples:

In this extract (and not others)
A detailed account (not a general analysis)
For what reasons (more than one)
Two separate scenes (not one).

Now we come to faults 3, 4 and 5, which are interrelated.

Fault Number Three: irrelevance. Often this is caused by faulty reading of the question but it can also be caused by the mistaken belief that very long answers are necessary. This happens because, often, the candidate feels he should give as much as he can. It is understandable, but the examiners require evidence of ability to see the point of a question, and answer accordingly. "Long irrelevant preambles and unpointed narrative demonstrated inability to answer questions" (Examiners' Report, 1985). Retelling of the entire story is a very common fault, when only one precise episode may be needed.

Fault Number Four: a misguided desire to reproduce material learnt by heart. When a candidate lacks confidence in his own ability, he prefers to rely on someone else's. This is disastrous, because it is hardly likely that such material is relevant to one particular question. "The writing-out of notes learnt by heart as an answer to any question on a book is always unsatisfactory" (Examiners' Report, 1981).

Fault Number Five: an inability to refer to the text properly. Most questions ask for "detail" and cannot be answered by unsupported opinion. Even if you are asked what you "feel" or what you "admire" or "like", your answer must be backed up by details from the book. Some students then try to quote at too great a length, and either waste too much time doing so, or become inaccurate. "Quotations could have been used more effectively. The point of a quotation is not made by the opening and closing words and a row of dots. An accurate and even simplified paraphrase shows more understanding than an ill-introduced half-remembered rehash of the text" (Examiners' Report, 1983). With a novel, especially, it is difficult to quote well. Do not attempt long quotations; keep them as brief as possible. Paraphrase means putting into your own words, and the examiners recommend it.

Analysing Examination Questions

"O" level questions tend to be very straightforward. They ask about characters, how characters relate to each other, or about episodes in the plot. They require a detailed knowledge, accurate description, and strict relevance. Questions about style, themes, structure and other generalities are not set, although an appreciation of these, in a simple way, is essential to your understanding of the book's overall value.

The more usual forms of questions are:
1. Give an account...
2. Describe the character of...

3. Trace the stage of...
4. How far do you think X is responsible for Y's misfortunes?
5. X said ... about Y. Why does he feel this way about him, and does he change his mind by the end of the novel?
6. By close reference to what X says and does in the novel, make clear why you find him an admirable/detestable character.
7. Show clearly the importance of: (e.g. in *Animal Farm*), physical appearance, food, ceremonies or ritual, speeches, physical description, the weather. (Usually only two or three topics or themes will be mentioned.)

It is important, when asked a "How far" or "To what extent" or "How important" type of question, to give a definite answer. Usually there are three choices in doing so: completely, not at all, or partly. You must state that you completely agree or disagree, or partly agree.

You are often asked to compare and contrast characters. Remember that *compare* means point out the similarities, whilst *contrast* means to point out the differences. Remember that your answer must show some organisation based on a five or six paragraph essay.

So, a series of "O" level type questions relating to *Animal Farm* might be like this:

1. Either (a) "The best way to read *Animal Farm* is not for the comments and lessons, but for the story and characters." Show how far you agree with this opinion by writing about *three* of your favourite animals as they appear in the novel.

   Or (b) By referring closely to *three* episodes in the novel, show that you have enjoyed *Animal Farm* not only for its story and characters, but also for its underlying satire.

2. Either (a) Choose *two* of the following: Napoleon, Boxer, Mollie, Squealer. Then (i) Write as vivid an

impression as you can of each of the two you choose,
illustrating your answer by reference to what they do
and say; *and* (ii) add a short paragraph for each of the
two animals, suggesting what you think Orwell is trying to tell us about human society through them.

Or (b) "And remember also in fighting against Man, we
must not come to resemble him. Even when you have conquered him, do not adopt his vices." Make clear
(i) how Old Major's warning was first taken seriously, by
describing the principles of Animalism as formulated by
the animals; *and* (ii) how later it was disregarded, by in-
dicating the actual state of affairs on the farm at the end
of the story.

Notice that these questions are fairly straightforward: they
ask you about characters, or about events in the story.

A typical question, with a suggested answer, follows. The
answer is based on the formula of an opening paragraph which
is a short answer to the question, supporting evidence in the
following paragraphs, and a conclusion which is more than
a limp re-statement of the question. Make a plan before you
start your answer.

Question

"By referring closely to *three* episodes in the novel, show
that you have enjoyed *Animal Farm* not only for its story
and characters, but also for its underlying satire."

First, note the key phrases, "not only" and "but also".
There are *two* parts to the question, and you cannot get
credit if you do not deal with "underlying satire" (the other
key words). You must "show" that you appreciate the
author's intention in mocking greed, exploitation, hypo-

crisy, gullibility, etc.. It is very common, in the rush of an examination, to forget the second part of the question and lose half the marks. That is why it is vital to make a plan, and a good tip is to make your first paragraph a summary of your entire answer. After all, you only have 30 minutes, and it would be a pity to lose marks because you spend so much time on describing the episodes and characters that you have no time to show that you understand the satire.

Notes

Which episodes? Select quickly. What you enjoyed may come to you straight away, but make sure you have enough to say about the episode, and that you understand the satire. Remember also that the term "enjoy" has a wide range of meanings, and need not refer only to lightly amusing episodes (like Mollie's vanity, or the cat trying to trap the sparrows) but to near tragic episodes like the death of Boxer or the executions. The fact that you have "enjoyed" them as literature does not mean that you sympathise any the less.

Some possibilities

1. Major's speech.
2. Snowball's rivalry with Napoleon.
3. The Battle of the Windmill.
4. The Animal Re-education Committee.
5. The expulsion of Snowball.
6. The confessions and executions.
7. The glorification of Napoleon as leader.
8. Napoleon outsmarted by Frederick.
9. Napoleon's hangover.
10. The death of Boxer.

You may decide to strike a balance between light and serious episodes, and so select and note:
1. The Animal Re-education Committee:
   comical, unrealistic, over-ambitious.
2. Napoleon as glorified leader:
   totally exaggerated; vanity and megalomania (power-madness).
3. The confessions and executions:
   very dramatic. Terror and "black" comedy (dealing with unpleasant realities in a cynical or macabre manner). Falseness of forced confessions.

The framework for your five-paragraph answer then becomes:
1. Summary of your answer.
2. Animal Re-education Committee.
3. Napoleon as glorified leader.
4. The confessions and executions.
5. Conclusion: light or sombre, a penetrating insight into human nature.

Answer

Orwell shows up the faults of individuals and the system in *Animal Farm*. In the Animal Committees episode he shows that it is unrealistic, for instance, to expect cats and sparrows to be friends because of the Wild Comrades Re-education Committee. Napoleon's love of glory is mocked by calling him "Ducklings' Friend" when he obviously is not, and so the title is ridiculous. Orwell's satire becomes much darker when animals are killed in a most brutal manner — by having their throats torn out. Here Orwell achieves "black" comedy — the serious injustice of executing innocent animals is highlighted by how comically inconsequential the offences are, such as urinating in the drinking pool. The characters of Snowball and Napoleon are brought out in these three episodes.

Snowball is an enthusiastic and energetic intellectual organiser, and Orwell mocks this mania for education in a gentle way. He admires Snowball's energy — he was "indefatigable in organizing committees" — and idealism, but some of Snowball's ideas are plainly unworkable, such as the "Whiter Wool Movement" for sheep. Snowball's mistaken belief that ordinary animals can be organised in such a way is bluntly labelled a "failure". Not every animal can think like an intellectual, and Snowball ignores basic instincts of nature — such as the cat's exploitation of the Wild Comrades Re-education Committee in order to try to get a good meal. The wild animals themselves "when treated with generosity, simply took advantage of it". Orwell is pointing out that changes can be made, but not in such a dramatic way as to go against basic human (or animal) nature.

The account of Napoleon's vanity mocks the self-importance of many dictators, who like to project an image of benevolent paternalism (that is, of a kindly father) despite their cruel and savage actions. The stupidity of the exploited is also shown by their gullible belief that Napoleon can actually help the hens to lay eggs, or improve the taste of the water, when clearly it has nothing to do with Napoleon. The honours bestowed on him are worthless, because they either originate from Napoleon himself (he awards himself medals, and makes himself President) or from the pigs who need to flatter Napoleon in order to stay alive. The sentimental image of kindliness ("Friend of the fatherless! Fountain of happiness!") is the very opposite of Napoleon's cruelty.

The confessions and executions satirise the absolute ruthlessness with which dictators eliminate opposition, not only by killing opponents (which could be done secretly), but by a public spectacle, to try to justify such killings, and also to terrify any other potential opposition. The satire is directed at the method of terror. The show of force by the dogs "sent shivers down all the animals' spines". Already, the atmosphere is set, and even the innocent animals feel threatened — no one is safe in such a situation. The details of the attack of the dogs on the young porkers and Boxer are shocking — "The pigs' ears were bleeding, the dogs had tasted blood, and for a few moments they appeared to go quite mad." Ironically, Orwell states that the porkers "waited, trembling, with guilt written on every line of their countenances". They were "trembling" in sheer terror, and had no choice but to confess. The fact that *all* opposition is intolerable is highlighted by the fact that the noble Boxer is one of the attacked, and that the other "confessions" are by harmless animals doing trivial things. The sheer magnitude of the purge is pictured in the "pile of corpses lying before Napoleon's feet" — so many sacrificed at the will of one.

All three episodes show us more about the faults of human nature, from the light, and harmless, zeal of Snowball (which is actually noble and well-intentioned) to the more blame-worthy vanity and lying of Napoleon, and then to the terrible blood-lust which is released to satisfy the power madness of an individual. Although all of these episodes are "enjoyable" in the sense that they reflect the failings of individuals, they also do teach us a moral lesson.

How to Write an Essay

How do I write an essay? The answer is to know the book thoroughly and to write relevantly. This means that you can know the book extremely well but fail because you do not pay close attention to how the question is worded. Always remember that there may be more than one aspect to an examination question. For example, when confronted with the question:

"The creatures outside looked from pig to man, and from man to pig ... but already it was impossible to say which was which." With reference to the quotation, trace the rise and fall of idealism in *Animal Farm*.

It is very easy to show how the pigs adopt human habits and vices, and there is so much material that you might get carried away and spend all your time writing about this. If you do, at the most you will get half the total marks. This is a common fault, because your attention is focused on the quotation, and you comment on that only, without tracing the "rise and fall of idealism" as it affects the other animals.

So first of all, you must understand the question and check whether there is (as in this example) more than one part to it. Secondly, you must decide quickly if you have enough material for your answer. You can jot down an outline to see if you have enough points and illustrations. If you have, you should plan your essay carefully.

This is extremely important. It is only human for candidates to feel pressured into scribbling down as much as they can, but the examiners are quite clear about what they want: "Examiners were all concerned about the unsatisfactory quality of the work in Section C and suggested ... that candidates be trained to organise their time more wisely in order to answer the essay question more fully, and that the candidates be given much needed practice in the actual techniques of essay-writing, of which at present, there is little evidence" ("N" level report 1986). "O" level examiners make much the same comment: "Further practice in the techniques of essay writing is obviously necessary.

There was far too much unthinking narrative here, with even some use of scrappy notes, and far too little evidence of *shaping* the required material'' (Report, 1985).

So remember — plan! You have a lot of information whirling around in your head and only 30 minutes for your answer. You must choose from your store of knowledge, and keep to the point. Do not try to impress the examiner, and reassure yourself, by scribbling a lot. A little time "lost" in preparation will gain you many more marks for clarity, logical arrangement, and relevance. Follow this plan:

First paragraph   : idealistic and exploitative types
Second paragraph : early idealism
Third paragraph   : gradual erosion of values
Fourth paragraph : final erosion of values
Fifth paragraph   : final state: complete disillusionment and corruption

First paragraph

Answer the question in general terms, as if it were a summary of the entire question:

Many of the animals, typified by Boxer and Clover, hold on to old Major's principles to the bitter end, while others (such as the four young porkers) are executed for raising objections. Boxer even burns his straw hat, because he sees it as a badge of slavery. The animals are uneasy about the milk and apples, dealings with humans, the killings, drinking alcohol and so on, but they have no effective leadership after the expulsion of Snowball. Snowball may have been able to stay closer to old Major's ideals than Napoleon, but it is clear by the end that not only have the pigs adopted the habits and vices of mankind, but they are worse: they tyrannise their own kind. This is old Major's most impor-

tant principle: "And above all, no animal must ever tyrannise his own kind." Some animals firmly believe in this, but in the end the pigs disregard it completely.

This type of opening paragraph should help you to keep your plan in mind; the examiner should be glad that you are not beating about the bush, and all you need now is some supporting detailed examples, and a neat conclusion. Should you run out of time before doing this, or your memory fail you, you have still answered the question. Not fully, agreed, but you have summarised your approach in the first paragraph, and will gain marks, whereas some long "answers" can be partly or totally irrelevant, and will be penalised accordingly.

Second paragraph (first in note form, then in continuous prose)

Early idealism shown in both theory and practice. Principles of Animalism set out by the pigs, who faithfully follow old Major's teachings in simplified form for the less intelligent. Do's and don'ts clearly formulated into seven commandments. Pigs also decide practical matters, like what to do with whips, farmhouse and ribbons. Leadership depends on intelligence, not morality. Early signs of corruption in disappearance of apples and milk. But work on farm goes well. Snowball and pigs help others to read. All strive for self-improvement. Idealism to include wild comrades. Co-operation in problem-solving, and in Battle. Democracy in meetings. Better living conditions envisaged.

There is a lot of material here, too much for an exam answer, so it must be condensed into one paragraph. Do not forget, either, the *link* between paragraphs. Conjunctions usually point the way an essay is going, and indicate a change of direction. "And so" and "Consequently" show the subject is being developed, continued smoothly; "But", "However", "On the other hand" indicate some change, contrast or difference. Sometimes your paragraphs can be linked simply to indicate order: "Firstly", "Secondly" etc., or, "At the beginning", "In the middle", "At the end of the book" etc.. So our second paragraph can be linked to the first with a simple phrase, e.g.:

At first there is early idealism in theory and practice. The principles of Animalism are thought out by the pigs, and they faithfully adapt old Major's teachings into the Seven Commandments. There is general agreement on what to do with ribbons ("badges of slavery") because of the principle "all animals should go naked". Decisions on the farmhouse, harness, whips and chains are by general agreement at regular, democratic meetings. Co-operation and happiness are evident ("The work of the farm went like clock-work") and there is a good attitude to work ("everyone worked according to his capacity"), to wild comrades, and to self-improvement. The animals are unified by their glorious victory at the Battle of the Cowshed.

Third paragraph

This is where we show the early signs of corruption, and we indicate a *contrast* with the paragraph link — "But", "however" or "on the other hand". The earliest sign that Major's principles are being broken is the disappearance of the milk. Even Snowball agrees to the inequality of apples and milk for pigs only. This is rapidly followed by the terror of Snowball's expulsion and the abolition of democratic meetings. To enforce this, there are executions, even though the commandment clearly says, "No animal shall kill another animal", which the pigs had originally said was an "unalterable law". Some of the earliest resolutions made by the animals, not to deal with humans, or engage in trade or money, are soon forgotten. The animals are disillusioned to some extent, but Boxer thinks the fault comes from within themselves, and Clover expresses the general acceptance of Napoleon's leadership. Yet you should note that you are not asked for the animals' reaction, or to comment on the methods by which the changes are implemented. So leave this out. Therefore, the third paragraph is:

But right from the start, the pigs abuse the principle of equality by taking the milk and apples, and give orders rather than share in physical work. They soon recognise that opposition must be eliminated and, following the expulsion of Snowball, democratic meetings are abolished and all decisions are made by the pigs. Ironically, the "unalterable law" that "no animal shall kill another animal" is altered by the addition of the words "without cause". Rapid changes are made to the original resolutions never to deal with humans, engage in trade, deal in money, occupy the farmhouse, or sleep on beds.

Fourth paragraph

The main point to make here is that the gradual erosion of values is completed to the extent that the pigs, originally told not to resemble man or "adopt his vices" become undistinguishable from him. The death of Boxer, and the purchase of alcohol from the sale of his body, is a terrible sign of corruption, but the negotiations with Frederick and Pilkington betray the revolution. The revisions of the revolutionary details, such as the name of the farm, the reverence for old Major and the equality of the term "comrade", are final signs that the animals are in a worse state than under the humans. Note that this last point is the main conclusion, so leave it for your final paragraph. For the fourth paragraph you might say:

By the end of the book, all the commandments are broken, and the pigs are undistinguishable from man when the other animals view them drinking, cheating and arguing with the humans at a drunken party. Worst of all, the pigs go on two legs and start to use whips on their "comrades". The other habits which distinguish man, like wearing clothes, listening to the radio and using the telephone, seem minor compared to this, yet they are clear violations of Major's instructions. The treatment of Boxer shows that loyalty is rewarded with treachery and cruelty, and far from the pigs having just a few privileges for their different needs and tastes, it demonstrates brutally how they have nothing in common with the other animals.

Fifth paragraph: The Conclusion

The conclusion is very important, and you should always try to make sure that you have something special to say to round off your essay. Often students just continue to give examples, or write until they run out of time. Be prepared to cut short your examples, leave out your favourite quote, or condense your other paragraphs, in order to make a special point in your conclusion, such as here — that the animals are not merely back in the same old position of hardship and cruelty, but *they are worse off*. Another important aspect of a conclusion, apart from summarising your entire argument, is to refer to the beginning, to give the essay balance and unity. Thus:

So we see that, in every way, the pigs have done exactly the opposite of what old Major had instructed. They exploit the other animals to the point of killing them. The chief human "vice" which Major had denounced was not alcohol, clothes or sleeping on a bed, bad as they are, but the inequality and injustice of the Master and Slave relationship. The clear rule that "Whatever goes on two legs is an enemy" is broken when the pigs imitate man in this most obvious way. The re-use of whips establishes the return of cruel slavery. The final irony is that the animals are now worse off than they were under their natural enemy, man. "no animal must tyrannize over his own kind". In the worst way possible, they have clearly demonstrated that "some animals are more equal than others". (Notice that this conclusion refers to the first paragraph, but also ends with something new.)

Of course, paragraphs four and five can be condensed into one paragraph, if you are short of time. The conclusion should focus on the words of the question, to ensure that the second part is answered.

Points to Remember

1. You cannot use *all* of your material — select quickly.
2. Quote, if possible, but not too much (in a question of this type, for instance, it would take too long to support every point made with quotations).
3. Essay structure:
   (a) Make your plan.
   (b) Make your first paragraph a summary of your entire essay.
   (c) Link your paragraphs using meaningful conjunctions.
   (d) Try for a neat conclusion.

Context Questions

"The textual question may require candidates to explain words or phrases, to rewrite passages in modern English, or to relate an extract to the work as a whole" ("O" level examination syllabus, 1988).

Context at "O" level requires a very detailed knowledge of the text. It is not possible to guess or write generally and hope to pass. At "N" level also, the examiners are quite clear: "Irrelevance was particularly prevalent ... candidates began the required accounts far too early, and thus wrote much for which little or no credit could be given. It also occurred in answers to 8 (b) where the words 'near the end of the novel' were taken as an invitation to describe the events at the end of the novel and not those asked for in the question" (Examiners Report, 1985). The question mentioned in the report was on *The Pearl*. Candidates were asked to "Describe what happened near the end of the novel when Kino left the cave where he, Juana and Coyotito were hiding, and attacked the three men who had followed them there". Obviously, the important thing is to concentrate on describing Kino's *attack* on the three men, not *everything* which happened near the end of the novel. This is a result of hasty reading, and seeing only the first few words of the question.

Another major fault noted by "N" level examiners is that "In answers to the first part of the context questions, candidates still tended to quote from the passage rather than to explain or make a deduction from it". This means that students use the words of the passage in their answer, instead of working out what the question is getting at and answering in their own words. Let us have a look at an "N" level-type example.

Context A

But just at that moment, as though at a signal, all the sheep burst out into a tremendous bleating of —

"Four legs good, two legs *better!* Four legs good, two legs *better!* Four legs good, two legs *better!*"

It went on for five minutes without stopping. And by the time the sheep had quieted down, the chance to utter any protest had passed, for the pigs had marched back into the farmhouse.

Benjamin felt a nose nuzzling at his shoulder. He looked round. It was Clover. Her old eyes looked dimmer than ever. Without saying anything, she tugged gently at his mane and led him round to the end of the big barn, where the Seven Commandments were written. For a minute or two they stood gazing at the tarred wall with its white lettering.

"My sight is failing", she said finally. "Even when I was young I could not have read what was written there. But it appears to me that that wall looks different. Are the Seven Commandments the same as they used to be, Benjamin?"

For once Benjamin consented to break his rule, and he read out to her what was written on the wall. There was nothing there now except a single Commandment. It ran:

ALL ANIMALS ARE EQUAL
BUT SOME ANIMALS ARE MORE
EQUAL THAN OTHERS

Questions

1. (a) What has happened immediately before this?
   (b) How long had it taken the sheep to learn this new slogan?
   (c) Does Clover show any anger? Explain.

(d) Give *two* examples of how particular commandments had been changed.

(e) What is Benjamin's usual rule?

2. Describe how the animals react to this new commandment.

Answers

1. (a) The pigs had appeared on two legs, with Napoleon carrying a whip.

(b) One week.

(c) No. Clover has a very gentle, trusting nature. She is very old, and used to disappointment. She has no fight left.

(d) No animal shall sleep in a bed "with sheets".

No animal shall drink alcohol "to excess".

(e) He seldom talked or read, because he said there was nothing worth reading.

2. The animals accept the new commandment as they have accepted things all along. Now they are in a state of shock in which their responses are dulled. Their first instinct on seeing the pigs on two legs, and Napoleon with a whip, was to protest, but they are prevented by the sheep bleating out the new slogan. After this terrible shock, anything seems acceptable; it does not seem strange to see the pigs carrying whips, wearing clothes, or even Napoleon smoking a pipe. When a group of humans come to inspect the farm, the animals do not know "whether to be more frightened of the pigs or of the human visitors". They observe the party in the farmhouse as spectators, not as participants. All they can do now is to watch passively.

Notice that these answers are brief: "Context questions normally ask for very precise information: general comment is irrelevant to such an answer" (Examiners Report, 1981). Therefore, do not be tempted to write too much. Get right to the point and leave it at that.

Do not worry if you do not get all of the points. You do not need all the marks to pass! In question 2 you are asked to write a "mini-essay" and since you are writing at greater length, be careful not to just scribble, but try to arrange your material in an orderly way. This question wants you to describe another part of the book, either before or after the passage. It has a link with the passage, of course, but you cannot hope to pass this section by relying on the passage printed in front of you.

The context at "O" level varies in form. In Section A (usually Shakespeare) it is very detailed, and similar to the "N" level type of context. In Section B, however, it is usually only one (or two) of the set texts which has a "context" passage, and it is of a different type. In this section, the questions are usually more general, using a passage as a starting point for a general appreciation of the novel. In 1985, the question on *Hard Times* by Dickens went, "This extract ... contains a great deal of material which one later realises to be of great significance, as regards character and theme. Make clear the significance of as much of this material as you can."

The examiners were disappointed that it "led to a paraphrase of the extract or to a general summary of the plot without making use of the material" (Report, 1985). The other context question in the same paper was from *Short Stories of Our Time* and had four detailed questions requiring a good knowledge of the whole story.

The essential skill in answering context questions is precision. This requires a very accurate *selection* of relevant details and explanations. The faults frequently noted are: over-generalisation (such as re-telling the whole plot), not knowing the precise details asked for, not focusing on the material provided. Let us have a look at both types of "O" level context questions.

Context B

Boxer professed not to be sorry for what had happened. If he made a good recovery, he might expect to live another three years, and he looked forward to the peaceful days that he would spend in the corner of the big pasture. It would be the first time that he had had leisure to study and improve his mind. He intended, he said, to devote the rest of his life to learning the remaining twenty-two letters of the alphabet.

However, Benjamin and Clover could only be with Boxer after working hours, and it was in the middle of the day when the van came to take him away. The animals were all at work weeding turnips under the supervision of a pig, when they were astonished to see Benjamin come galloping from the direction of the farm buildings, braying at the top of his voice. It was the first time that they had ever seen Benjamin excited — indeed, it was the first time that anyone had ever seen him gallop. "Quick, quick!" he shouted. "Come at once! They're taking Boxer away!" Without waiting for orders from the pig, the animals broke off work and raced back to the farm buildings. Sure enough, there in the yard was a large closed van, drawn by two horses, with lettering on its side and a sly-looking man in a low-crowned bowler hat sitting on the driver's seat. And Boxer's stall was empty.

The animals crowded round the van. "Good-bye, Boxer!" they chorused, "good-bye!"

Questions

1. Why had Boxer not learnt more than four letters of the alphabet?
2. How had the pigs helped Boxer during his illness?
3. What is Benjamin's normal manner?
4. What is Benjamin's reaction to the animals saying good-bye?
5. What is Squealer's version of what happens to Boxer after this?

Answers

1. He was not clever and could not remember any more without forgetting the first four he had learnt.
2. They had sent a large bottle of pink medicine.
3. He is normally quiet, cynical, unsociable, obstinate and slow.
4. He is angry. He calls them fools because they do not realise that Boxer is going, not to the vet, but to the knacker's.
5. Squealer claims that Boxer died in hospital, uttering revolutionary slogans like "Napoleon is always right" as his final words. He explains that the knacker's van has been bought by the vet, who has not had time to remove the knacker's name from it. He exaggerates the care and cost that Napoleon contributed to Boxer's treatment.

Context C

All through that summer the work of the farm went like clockwork. The animals were happy as they had never conceived it possible to be. Every mouthful of food was an acute positive pleasure, now that it was truly their own food, produced by themselves and for themselves, not doled out to them by a grudging master. With the worthless parasitical human beings gone, there was more for everyone to eat. There was more leisure too, inexperienced though the animals were. They met with many difficulties — for instance, later in the year, when they harvested the corn, they had to tread it out in the ancient style and blow away the chaff with their breath, since the farm possessed no threshing machine — but the pigs with their cleverness and Boxer with his tremendous muscles always pulled them through. Boxer was the admiration of everybody. He had been a hard worker even in Jones's time, but now he seemed more like three horses than one; there were days when the entire work of the farm seemed to rest upon his mighty shoulders. From morning to night he was pushing and pulling, always at the spot where the work was hardest. He had made an arrangement with one of the cockerels to call him in the mornings half an hour earlier than anyone else, and would put in some volunteer labour at whatever seemed to be most needed, before the regular day's work began. His answer to every problem, every setback, was "I will work harder!" — which he had adopted as his personal motto.

Question

The above extract is from the early part of *Animal Farm*, and contains a great deal of material which we later realise is of considerable significance, as regards both character and theme. Make clear the significance of as much of this material as you can.

Answer

This passage clearly shows the idealism of the farm in the

early days, and a brief period of happiness for the animals before disillusionment and hardship set in. At this point, there is co-operation in work, plenty of food, no cruelty, time for leisure, and the challenge of overcoming problems. The passage highlights the contrasting themes of exploitation, gullibility and corruption which are dealt with later. There is no reason why the farm should not continue to exist happily, but the pigs are so greedy for power that they exploit the gullible animals by reducing their food and freedom, and increasing their workload and hardships. We see the point that there is enough for everyone to share but that the happiness of the majority is sacrificed to the pigs.

Boxer's character is portrayed in detail in this passage. It is admirable, but his lack of intelligence allows him to be easily exploited. His motto of "I will work harder!" is not always the right solution, as we see later. His adoption of slogans leads to disaster, especially the slogan "Napoleon is always right". Boxer has great integrity, and stands up for Snowball, until Squealer uses Napoleon's name. It is only later that we realise that these tremendous sacrifices by Boxer are not rewarded. Worse than that, there is an attempt to kill him when he defends Snowball, and in the end he is sold off to the knacker.

The mention of the pigs' cleverness is quite neutral at this point, and we have no hint as to how they will later abuse their ability at the expense of the other animals.

This answer may be a bit long if only 30 minutes are available, but it does answer the question. It *selects* important details from the passage, and relates them *briefly* to the later developments in the novel. It does not paraphrase or generalise too much, and makes use frequently of the key words "significance", "later", "character", and "theme".

Other context questions for practice:

Context D

Once again the animals were conscious of a vague uneasiness. Never to have any dealings with human beings, never to engage in trade, never to make use of money — had not these been among the earliest resolutions passed at that first triumphant Meeting after Jones was expelled? All the animals remembered passing such resolutions: or at least they thought that they remembered it. The four young pigs who had protested when Napoleon abolished the Meetings raised their voices timidly, but they were promptly silenced by a tremendous growling from the dogs. Then, as usual, the sheep broke into "Four legs good, two legs bad!" and the momentary awkwardness was smoothed over. Finally Napoleon raised his trotter for silence and announced that he had already made all the arrangements. There would be no need for any of the animals to come in contact with human beings, which would clearly be most undesirable. He intended to take the whole burden upon his own shoulders. A Mr Whymper, a solicitor living in Willingdon, had agreed to act as intermediary between Animal Farm and the outside world, and would visit the farm every Monday morning to receive his instructions. Napoleon ended his speech with his usual cry of "Long live Animal Farm!", and after the singing of "Beasts of England" the animals were dismissed.

Questions

1. Why had Napoleon decided to engage in trade, and what *three* commodities did he propose to sell?
2. Why had the Meetings been abolished, and what happened to the four young pigs?

3. Which animals (apart from the pigs) come into contact with the outside world?
4. How does Squealer set the animals' minds at rest?
5. What is the result of the trade with Frederick?

Context E

On Sundays there was no work. Breakfast was an hour later than usual, and after breakfast there was a ceremony which was observed every week without fail. First came the hoisting of the flag. Snowball had found in the harness-room an old green tablecloth of Mrs Jones's and had painted on it a hoof and a horn in white. This was run up the flagstaff in the farmhouse garden every Sunday morning. The flag was green, Snowball explained, to represent the green fields of England, while the hoof and horn signified the future Republic of the Animals which would arise when the human race had been finally overthrown. After the hoisting of the flag all the animals trooped into the big barn for a general assembly which was known as the Meeting. Here the work of the coming week was planned out and resolutions were put forward and debated. It was always the pigs who put forward the resolutions. The other animals understood how to vote, but could never think of any resolutions of their own. Snowball and Napoleon were by far the most active in the debates. But it was noticed that these two were never in agreement: whatever suggestion either of them made, the other could be counted on to oppose it. Even when it was resolved — a thing no one could object to in itself — to set aside a small paddock behind the orchard as a home of rest for animals who were past work, there was a stormy debate over the correct retiring age for each class of animal. The Meeting always ended with the singing of "Beasts of England", and the afternoon was given up to recreation.

Question

The extract contains a good deal of material which one later realises to be of great significance. Make clear the significance of as much of this material as you can.

Revision Questions

1. Orwell slips into the world of the animal fable in his second paragraph, casually introducing the fact that his animals can talk with: "Word had gone round during the day ..." What human characteristics — other than speech — has Orwell given to:

Old Major	Mollie	Snowball
Boxer	Benjamin	Napoleon

2. Why was old Major so respected by all the animals on the farm? What noble ideals are set forth in his dream? Why are the animals so excited by their singing of "Beasts of England"?

3. The take-over of the rebellion by the pigs is similar to the way in which the Russian Revolution was taken over by a small, organised group, the Bolsheviks. In Orwell's fable, why were the pigs accepted as leaders by the other animals? What particular motive did the pigs have in bringing about the rebellion?

4. Who formulated the Seven Commandments? Were they arrived at in a democratic way? How well do they reflect the ideals expressed in old Major's speech?

5. **Foreshadowing.** Storytellers often arouse curiosity and expectation in their readers by hinting at later events or raising unsolved questions or mysteries.

For instance, at the end of Chapter Two, " ... it was noticed that the milk had disappeared." How does this mysterious disappearance foreshadow future events on the farm?

6. **Semantics.** The study of the meanings of language is called semantics. One of the chief themes of *Animal Farm* is the pigs' manipulation of language to confuse and control the other animals. What are some ways in which the pigs make clever use of language in Chapter Three in order to gain their own ends?

7. In the first months after the rebellion, how are the animals better off than they had been under Jones? Are they worse off in any ways? Explain.

8. After the Russian Revolution, the Soviets next set about to extend their Revolution throughout the world. How do the pigs try to extend their rebellion? What is their plan for domination of the surrounding farms?

9. Who leads the animals to victory at the Battle of the Cowshed? What human reactions do some of the animals have to the battle? What human rituals do they use to celebrate their victory?

10. **Character.** What kind of "person" is Mollie? How and why does she betray the ideals of Animal Farm? What does the story of Mollie suggest about the relation of the individual to any system of government?

11. **Significant Detail.** What is suggested by this description of the dogs' behaviour towards Napoleon: "It was noticed that they wagged their tails to him in the same way as the other dogs had been used to do with Mr Jones"? What later events are foreshadowed by this detail?

12. **Character.** Why does Napoleon change his position on the building of the windmill? What does this episode show about him?

13. How does Napoleon use the building of the windmill to strengthen his control over the other animals? How is history twisted when Snowball is mentioned?

14. Chapter Seven contains some strong examples of the gullibility of human nature. Which events in this chapter show how unscrupulous leaders can manipulate the minds of those who trust them?

15. **Irony.** Irony is achieved by saying or writing the opposite of what is really meant. What irony do you find in the following passage:
"As Clover looked down the hillside her eyes filled with tears ... they had come to a time when no one dared speak his mind, when fierce, growling dogs roamed everywhere, and when you had to watch your comrades torn to pieces after confessing to shocking crimes ... She knew that, even as things were, they were far better off than they had been in the days of Jones ..."

16. **Inference.** An inference is a conclusion or conjecture drawn from facts. Orwell does not tell us why Napoleon bans the singing of "Beasts of England"; he leaves it for us to *infer*. What conclusions do you draw about Napoleon's motives for banning the song?

17. How does Napoleon's behaviour at the Battle of the Windmill compare with Snowball's behaviour at the Battle of the Cowshed? Who is a better leader? Who is a better politician? Why?

18. By the end of Chapter Eight, how has the difference between the pigs and the other animals increased?

19. Why do the pigs encourage Moses to stay on the farm and tell his tales even though they claim that they are lies?

20. What happens to Boxer? How does Squealer explain away this great betrayal? Why do the animals accept

his explanation? What do the pigs gain from the transaction?

21. **Significant detail.** What is significant about Napoleon's changing the farm's name back to Manor Farm? How does this change symbolise what has happened in the story?

22. What are the final betrayals of Old Major's dream?

23. How does the final image of the novel — the pigs and men sitting together inside the house — sum up the meaning of *Animal Farm?*

24. How has Orwell used the animal fable to present his view of human nature? Back up any generalisations you make with specific scenes and characters from *Animal Farm*.

25. With what ideas and which characters is Orwell most in sympathy? What are some of the ways in which he shows his sympathy?

26. A famous philosopher, Hegel, once said: "The people arc that part of a State that does not know what it wants." Several times in the story, the animals would like to protest against unfair changes that the pigs are forcing on them, but they do not. What prevents them from doing so? What qualities does Orwell suggest are necessary for those who would remain free men?

27. Choose *one* of the following quotations and discuss it in relation to *Animal Farm:*

    (a) "All power tends to corrupt, but absolute power corrupts absolutely." (Lord Acton)

    (b) "Children and subjects are much seldomer in the wrong than parents and kings."(Lord Chesterfield)

Examination Questions

1. Benjamin is very intelligent; Boxer is stupid. Why are they good friends?
2. Compare and contrast the song "Beasts of England" with the poem "Comrade Napoleon".
3. How are the chapters linked to each other?
4. Is it better to have stupid rulers who are honest, or clever rulers who are dishonest? Answer with detailed reference to *Animal Farm*.
5. What elements make *Animal Farm* a fairy story?
6. Give an account of the two Battles. In what ways do they differ?
7. What part do the humans play in *Animal Farm?* Are they any better or worse than the pigs?
8. What animals are vain and selfish? Give reasons or examples in support of your answer.
9. Which scene do you consider to be
   (a) the most moving scene;
   (b) the most horrific;
   (c) the most amusing?
10. What different forms of humour are there in *Animal Farm?*
11. Give an account of the opening scene where Major gives his speech.
12. Why does the opening scene begin and close with Mr Jones the farmer?
13. How is Major's memory
    (a) preserved;
    (b) erased?
14. *Animal Farm* is a story of broken promises, some serious and some minor. Give three examples of each kind.

15. What might have happened if Snowball had been allowed to stay?
16. What is more important to the animals: memories of the past, or hope for the future? Give reasons in support of your answer.
17. How are the animals compensated for their hardships?
18. Speech-making is very important in *Animal Farm*. Compare the effectiveness of the various speechmakers.
19. Would young children understand the ending of the story? Is it necessary to have a happy ending?
20. In what ways are the animals worse off at the end than they were in the beginning?

HISTORICAL REFERENCES

Stalin (1879-1953)

Stalin's real name was Joseph Vissarionovich Dzhugashvili, but he became known as Stalin, "Man of Steel". Known for his cold ruthlessness and brutality, an early incident in prison shows his self-control: "He had to be flogged for preaching rebellion to the other prisoners. He presented himself — reading one of his books. The blows fell — he continued to read. Ordered to lay down his book, he merely went on reading. The book was torn from his hand and thrown on the floor, and the last lashes laid on. He neither winced nor cried out, though they were savage enough. And when it was all over and his hands were freed, he stooped down, picked up his book — resumed reading as though what had happened had been merely a trivial interruption" (G. Sava, *One Russian's Story*). This shows how he was gradually creating the image of a "Man of Steel".

Orwell chooses to satirise Stalin by calling him "Napoleon". Napoleon Bonaparte (1769-1821), General and Emperor of France, betrayed the French Revolution (1789) which was based on Equality, Liberty, and Brotherhood. After the Reign of Terror (with which he was associated) he seized power in 1799. He became Consul for life in 1802, and crowned himself Emperor in 1804. A brilliant General who ruled much of Europe after a series of great victories, he was defeated by the harsh Russian winter in his attempt on Russia (1812) and was finally defeated by the British at Waterloo in 1815. "To meet your Waterloo" is now a proverbial phrase meaning that proud and over-reaching people will one day be humbled. "Power is my mistress," said Bonaparte, "I love it as a musician loves his violin; I love it as an artist." As one historian put it, Napoleon might have added, "The artist dare not lend his violin, and least of all to an incompetent player ..." The great man had no intention of sharing power, least of all with the people.

The educational system was designed to produce propaganda favourable to the Emperor. One of his better known remarks on education was "Young people can hardly avoid accepting whatever version of the facts is presented to them".

The free expression of opinion was not tolerated in Napoleonic France. "I shall never allow the press to say anything contrary to my interests."

The comparison is rather strange, because Napoleon and Stalin were very different personalities. Both were absolute dictators who achieved a tremendous amount by far-sighted and ruthless methods. Napoleon established a legal code, which still exists in France today, and is the model for many other countries. Stalin dragged Russia out of the Middle Ages to be a World Industrial Power. Napoleon had great personal charm and was often kind, even to enemies. Napoleon is still a hero in France. Stalin executed people who had helped him to power, and, ironically, his achievement has now been "revised" by a process of "de-Stalinisation". His body was removed from its place of honour alongside Lenin. Yet it is undeniable that Stalin, like Napoleon, had hypnotic charm. Modern poet Yevtushenko illustrates this: "Many genuine Bolsheviks who were arrested at that time utterly refused to believe that this happened with his knowledge, still less on his personal instructions. They wrote to him. Some of them, after being tortured, inscribed "Long Live Stalin" in their blood on the walls of their prison. Secondly, in the minds of Soviet people, Stalin's name was indissolubly linked with Lenin's. Stalin knew how popular Lenin was and saw to it that history was re-written in such a way as to make his own relations with Lenin seem much closer than ever they were in fact. The re-writing was so thorough that perhaps Stalin himself believed his own version in the end" (From Yevtushenko's *A Precocious Autobiography*).

V. I. Lenin (1870-1924)

Lenin influenced Communism more than anyone else except Karl Marx. He adapted Marxist theory to the realities of Russia's backward economy, and displayed a continuing hope of world-wide socialist revolution by founding the Comintern (Communist International). He wanted Trotsky to succeed him, and warned against Stalin's growing ambition for power. He suffered a series of strokes and died in 1924, when his leadership was universally respected by all the various factions. Although revered in his own time, and now treated like an infallible God in Russia and other communist countries, he was far from perfect (at least from a Marxist point of view). He did not practise true equality, for instance, and believed that The Party (a privileged elite, to which the ordinary mass of people could not belong) would lead the revolution and direct it afterwards.

Leon Trotsky (1879-1940)

Trotsky believed in world-wide revolution, and so was bitterly opposed to Stalin's isolationist policy of "Socialism in one country". Brilliant but arrogant, Trotsky was a figure of heroic proportions — the leading public figure of the Bolshevik Revolution, organiser of the Red Army, later (exiled by Stalin for urging a more revolutionary, democratic policy) the founder of an international opposition to Stalinism. Although more sympathetic to Trotsky than Stalin, George Orwell was never a Trotskyite, because although Trotsky was unmistakably the mortal enemy of the Napoleonic *dictator,* he never relinquished the idea of the disciplined centralised party which would lead the workers. Orwell believed in power in the hands of the workers. Trotsky was assassinated in Mexico City in 1940.

Karl Marx (1818-1883)

Marx was a German philosopher who, together with Engels, wrote the *Communist Manifesto* in 1848 (a year of revolutions). This calls upon the proletariat (the workers) to rebel and overthrow the capitalists and bourgeoisie (the middle class)."Let the ruling classes tremble at a communist revolution. The proletarians have nothing to lose but their chains. They have a world to win. Workers of the world unite!"

The Russian Revolution

Actually, there were two Russian revolutions in 1917. The first, in March, overthrew the Tsarist monarchy. Russia had had to mobilise population and resources to sustain the war effort. The Tsar, Nicholas II, had assumed command at the front and virtually abandoned the government of the country to the nervous and hysterical Tsarina, who had fallen under the influence of Rasputin. This charlatan, posing as a Holy Man, was now directing affairs of State.

As Russia's military disasters mounted, so did evidence of corruption and inefficiency. Transportation and communications, uncertain to begin with, broke down, creating a severe scarcity of food in the cities. Bread riots and street demonstrations broke out in Petrograd; soldiers sent to quell them refused to fire on the demonstrators. In December 1916, five conspirators murdered Rasputin. In March 1917 Nicholas II abdicated, and a coalition of liberal and democratic leaders hastily formed a Provisional Government. The Allied countries hailed the making of a new and democratic Russia. And the Provisional Government committed itself to continuing the War.

Tragically, the new government failed to grasp the true mood of the masses — the land hunger of the peasants and, above all, the overwhelming desire for peace. A rival power, the "soviets" — councils of workers and soldiers — grew up in several cities to challenge the Provisional Government. In the Petrograd Soviet the most extreme, militant Marxists, the Bolsheviks, gained the majority.

By tireless work and shrewd manoeuvres on the part of V. I. Lenin, the Bolsheviks captured the Revolution. Before the War, despairing of reform in Russia, Lenin had exiled himself in Switzerland. In his view the War was flatly capitalist and imperialist. The capitalist powers had parcelled out the world among themselves, he preached, and a dissatisfied power like Germany could seek a reapportionment of the colonial spoils only through war. The workers of the world had nothing to gain from the War, and there was no difference between the absolutism of the German Kaiser and the imperial repression practised by the British and the French capitalists. The only path to peace and emancipation, he asserted, lay through revolution. Turn the imperialist war into a civil war, he demanded.

Lenin's ambitions for revolution in Russia appealed to the Germans; he could be used against the Provisional Government, and thus against the Allies. The German government therefore arranged Lenin's return to Russia.

Back in Russia, Lenin raised the slogan of "Peace, land and bread", and it was popular. He organised the Bolsheviks in Petrograd and other cities and called for a revolutionary transfer of power to the soviets, denouncing all other parties in the government.

On the 7th of November 1917, the Bolsheviks arrested members of the Provisional Government and proclaimed a socialist State. It was a momentous date in world history. A small band of conspirators had successfully executed a revolution in the name of 145 million oppressed people under a banner proclaiming the cause of world revolution. By its attack upon imperialism, its denunciation of the War and its promises of peace and "democracy", the Bolshevik Revolution also held a dazzling appeal to colonial peoples.

In this way Russia became the capital of world Communism. One of the first acts of the new regime was to pull out of World War I. The Bolsheviks pledged to liberate the workers from capitalist exploitation and to distribute land to the peasants. They proclaimed the equality of all peoples in Russia.

In sharp contrast to the rest of the world, Communist Russia escaped the business slump and unemployment of the Depression (1929-39). Russia had been cut off from world trade since the Revolution. Ironically, it emerged an industrial giant in the very years when Western industry lay crippled.

During this period Russia was ruled with an iron fist by Joseph Stalin, a former theology student who had been expelled from school for insubordination. He had since become a Marxist and a professional revolutionary. When Lenin died in 1924, a power struggle ensued in the Communist Party Politburo, and Stalin won. Trostsky was sent into exile. In 1928, having taken over control of the government, he launched a programme of building "socialism in one country" — putting aside the Marxist principle of world revolution. He established an elaborate central planning apparatus with a highly complex bureaucracy. Instituting the first of several Five-Year Plans by which he aimed to industrialise Russia, he pushed the country to surpass the capitalist countries of the world.

In 1929 Stalin stated: "We are advancing full steam ahead along the path of industrialisation to Socialism, leaving behind the age-long Russian 'backwardness'. We are becoming a country of metal, a country of automobiles, a country of tractors. And when we have put the Soviet Union in a motor-car and the peasant in a tractor ... we shall see which countries may then be classified as backward and which as advanced".

Stalin's Five-Year Plans set ambitious goals. The object was to transform the economic and social character of the country without foreign help, and this was to be done by strict government supervision of industry and agriculture. The people of Russia were to work hard at low wages and to look to the future for their reward. Collective farms were set up to be tilled jointly by the peasants who lived on them, with farm machinery provided by the State. In the cities the government created and maintained new industries, into which it absorbed great numbers of new workers. Between 1926 and 1939, 20 million people moved from the country to the towns to take industrial jobs. Workers were paid according to their output. Wages varied according to the job, but there were no paupers and no very rich people. The first Five-Year Plan was followed by a second in 1933. Together the plans pushed Russia into the industrial age and created an exhilarating feeling that all were working in concert to build a glorious socialist State.

But the costs in human life, freedom and well-being were staggering. In the relentless drive to build an industrial State overnight, Russian workers laboured long hours for poor pay, lived in cramped, unheated quarters and had to forgo things that Westerners take for granted — shoes, radios, even food. They had to live with the system whether they liked it or not.

To protest was futile. Stalin and his henchmen brutally repressed whatever real or imagined opposition they encountered. Factories and farms were given production quotas they had to meet. The Party rulers blamed "wreckers", "foreign spies" and "imperialist agents" for the failure of a factory to produce its quota of ball bearings, or of a farm to grow its quota of wheat. The failure often cost the plant or farm manager his job — and sometimes his life. Landowning peasants who resisted the taking over of their farms were herded into concentration camps; within five years one million of these kulaks (peasants working for their own profit) were put to death or sent to labour camps in Siberia, together with four million members of their families.

Stalin dealt even more fiendishly with political opposition. In 1936, charging that treason had been uncovered, he set in motion a series of notorious purge trials. After publicising the luckless men's "confessions", Stalin had them put to death. In the army alone he liquidated some 400 officers from colonel upwards — more than half the officers of the army.

More purges followed in 1937 and 1938. By such methods he surrounded himself with "yes-men" who could be counted on to do his bidding.

Thanks to Stalin's reign of terror, the Five-Year Plans succeeded in their tremendous undertaking — in so far as their objective was to industrialise the nation. Though food, shoes and housing remained in short supply, the plans gave aeroplanes, railways, tractors and army tanks to Russia in an abundance that staggered those who could remember Russia prior to Stalin's advent. In the 10 years of the first two Five-Year Plans, Russia had the fastest industrial growth of any country in the world at that time.

By 1939 the Soviet Union had become a powerful industrial State, surpassed in production only by the United States and Germany. It had industrialised by its own efforts, without dependence on private enterprise and without foreign capital. Total economic planning, never explicit in the doctrines of Karl Marx, was put into practice by the Russian Communists.

In addition to industrialising, the Soviet Union made great strides in education under the Five-Year Plans, so that by 1941, 85 per cent of the country was literate.

Russian accomplishments in the face of an otherwise world-wide depression enhanced the prestige of the Soviet Union. Many who did not like its methods envied the results. Even in the United States and Western Europe, the attractions of Communism seemed strong to those who suffered disillusionment in the Depression.

FOR THE ADVANCED STUDENT

Utopian and Anti-Utopian Fiction

The tradition of utopian fiction — fiction that assumes the possibility of a perfect existence for man — is very old, as old as the story of the Garden of Eden in Genesis, at least for the Western world. It embodies both nostalgia for a legendary Golden Age and hope for the way man might live in some distant future.

Although *The Republic* of Plato is older, the name for this kind of fiction comes from Sir Thomas More's *Utopia*, published in Latin in 1516. In it a character discovers a land called Utopia, or Nowhere Land. A popular work, it was translated into English in 1551, and has since served as a model for writers who share More's purpose. Francis Bacon's *The New Atlantis* (1626) and Jonathan Swift's *Gulliver's Travels* (1726) are further examples of utopian novels.

The nineteenth century was particularly interested in the idea of utopia, both in literature and in social experiments. In English literature there are books like Samuel Butler's *Erewhon* — "nowhere" spelled backwards — (1872) and William Morris's *News from Nowhere* (1891). Tennyson, in "Locksley Hall" (1842), writes of seeing a "Vision of the world" in which, finally, man learns to live at peace with himself in a "Federation of the world".

In American literature, Edward Bellamy's *Looking Backward* (1888) and Herman Melville's *Typee* (1846) and *Omoo* (1847) are examples of the same impulse to see man in an uncorrupted state. This desire is related to the phenomenon of the frontier in American history. The West allowed the possibility of establishing an ideal society or community free of the historical evils that man had always suffered in Europe. When the peaceful community that Huckleberry Finn and his companion Jim establish on the raft is disrupted by the world, Huck eventually decides to "light out for the Territory". Twain accurately reflects, in *The Adventures of Huckleberry Finn* (1884), the impulse to flee to the frontier and away from civilisation. This is echoed in our own time in Holden Caulfield's desire to establish a community of the innocent somewhere in the West, in J. D. Salinger's *The Catcher in the Rye*.

In *Gulliver's Travels* (1726), Swift addresses the condition of and prognosis for the human race.

In parts one and two the little and big people, so clearly versions of ourselves, show us the relativity of our standards. Gulliver, another version of us, shows the relativity of our motives too. In Lilliput, while effortlessly admired and respected, he nonchalantly performs heroic exploits and insists on preserving a conquered people's liberty. In Brobdingnag, persecuted by pets and servants, he becomes a show-off eager to see a people's liberty crushed by cannon. Part three hits out in several directions: at colonial power, pedantry, and abstract learning. Gulliver reaches an impasse when he meets the Struldbruggs, people exempt from natural death: he has heard of their existence rapturously, as a longed-for means of improving or perfecting the human lot (only, of course, it is his own potential gain that he rhapsodises over), and, once disillusioned, he has nowhere else to turn.

Part four presents us with beings which look human but are loathsomely subhuman, and beings which look like horses but which offer the lure of a new ideal. The Houyhnhnms' perfect rationality is genuinely impressive, but they are also funny, with their neighing language and gawky equine *politesse*. Gulliver has never appeared so ludicrous on his earlier voyages as here, from the beginning, when he is frisked by an enquiring hoof, to the end, when he signalises his new adoption of perfect reason by loving the *smell* of English horses. We leave him convinced that he has attained a nature above the human.

In *Brave New World* by Aldous Huxley (1932), people in the hatchery are mass-produced by artificial insemination and chemically conditioned to fit into the rigidly ordered hierarchy that society has become.

From the foetal stage on, people are to take their pre-destined places in a society that ranges from Alpha Plus, the highly intelligent leaders, to Epsilon Minus Semi Morons, the ill-shaped, ape-like goons who do the dirty work.

The title of the novel describes a future that is anything but brave. Unable to face realistically such facts of life as pain, grief, and death, protected against anything disagreeable by the ever-present soma (a drug), living for the sensation of the moment, the people of Huxley's brave new world are a grotesque projection of "civilised" life in the 1920's.

Nineteen Eighty-Four by George Orwell (1948), as its title implies, is Orwell's version of the future awaiting mankind. A ceaseless, pointless war goes rumbling on, a war in which Oceania is in alliance with Eastasia against Eurasia. Though the war is unending, and the population continually stimulated by news of overwhelming victory or sensational defeat, nothing actually happens. A daily Two Minutes' Hate, directed against the mythical Goldstein (a Trotsky or Snowball figure), distracts people from their sufferings. Everything is controlled by the Party, which is itself controlled by the secret Inner Party; the Party's three slogans are "War Is Peace", "Freedom Is Slavery", and "Ignorance is Strength".

Orwell's central character, Winston Smith, works in the Ministry of Truth, where his job is largely the rewriting of history to suit the shifts of Party policy and removing from previous records the names of persons who have since been "vaporised". In secret revolt against the Party and his own miserable life, he permits himself the folly of being attracted to Julia.

They conspire against the Party and, believing on very little evidence that a fellow member of their staff — a senior called O'Brien — is also a revolutionary, they confide in him. O'Brien proves to be a pillar of the existing order, and Winston is imprisoned, beaten, and tortured until all resistance is burned out of him, and he finally betrays Julia, who has already betrayed him.

This is what happens if the state is allowed to become all-powerful.

In *Nineteen Eighty-Four,* Orwell took care to see that his ruling elite was well motivated. "Why should we want power?" O'Brien demands of Winston. Winston's answer is unsatisfactory, and O'Brien supplies the true one:

Party seeks power entirely for its own sake. We are not interested in the good of others; we are interested solely in power. Not wealth or luxury or long life or happiness; only power, pure power ... Power is not a means; it is an end. One does not establish a dictatorship in order to safeguard a revolution; one makes the revolution in order to establish the dictatorship. The object of persecution is persecution. The object of torture is torture. The object of power is power. Now do you begin to understand me?

Political Allegory

An allegory is a story which has a meaning behind the surface meaning.

In Swift's *Gulliver's Travels* (1726) and George Orwell's *Animal Farm* (1945), both writers use allegory not to point to some greater truth but for the purpose of political and social comment. They tell bizarre stories, involving absurd and corrupt characters, but we can see that there are disturbing parallels with the real events of their day. Allegory of this kind is a favourite mode of present-day writers in countries where free speech is restricted and where any political comment has to be veiled and indirect.

When one studies the allegorical details of the book, the events of *Animal Farm* are transformations of the events of the Russian Revolution.

Orwell said that, in basing the book on the actual history of the Russian Revolution, he changed their chronological order. Changes include the omission of a Lenin figure. Major is Marx, Napoleon Stalin, and Snowball Trotsky. Lenin, the combination of idealist and prototypical totalitarian, is a complex personality with a complex role. Since Orwell wished to emphasise idealism's degeneration into tyranny, a figure combining both elements, rather than embodying one or the other, would demand the novel's resources of complexity and not the fable's simplifications. The omission of complex characters like Lenin greatly helps the symmetry of the story.

Major's speech is an accurate exposition of orthodox Marxism and is very similar to the last paragraph of the *Communist Manifesto* (1848). The Communists openly declare that their ends can be attained only by the forcible overthrow of all existing social conditions. Let the ruling class tremble at the Communistic revolution. The proletarians have nothing to lose but their chains. They have a world to win.

Marx stated, "From each according to his abilities, to each according to his needs"; and when Animal Farm is established, "everyone worked according to his capacity".

Although various episodes are taken from the actual history of the Russian Revolution, they are dealt with schematically and their chronological order is changed. The animals are Communists, the wild creatures who could not be tamed and are the *muzhiks* or peasants, the pigs are the Bolsheviks, the Rebellion is the October Revolution of 1917, the neighbouring farmers are the western armies who attempted to support the Tsarists against the Reds, the hoof and horn are the hammer and sickle, the special pig committee presided over by Napoleon is the Politburo.

The carefully chosen names are both realistic and highly suggestive of their owners' personalities and roles in the fable. The imperious Major (Marx-Lenin) is military, dominant and senior, the rather stupid and self-sacrificing Boxer (the proletariat), who is contrasted with the cynical Benjamin and the indifferent and unenthusiastic cat, is named after the Chinese revolutionaries who drove out foreign exploiters and were themselves crushed; Mollie (the White Russians) suggests folly; Moses brings divine law to man; Squealer (a living *Pravda*) is onomatopoetic for a voluble, propagandist pig; and Whymper, the pigs' agent, suggests a toady. Pilkington (Churchill-England), the capitalist exploiter, connotes "bilk" and "milk" (slang): he is an old-fashioned gentleman who enjoys country sports on Foxwood, which has associations of both craftiness and the Tory landed gentry. Frederick (Hitler) refers to Frederick the Great, the founder of the Prussian military state and Hitler's hero.

Like Trotsky, Orwell compares Stalin to Napoleon, for both turned revolutions into dictatorships, both transformed a national popular "revolution from below" into a foreign conqueror's "revolution from above", and both forcibly imposed their revolutionary ideologies on other countries.

The name Snowball recalls Trotsky's white hair and beard, and the fact that he melted before Stalin's opposition.

Two of the most important battles between Trotsky and Stalin are allegorised in the novel. Trotsky fought for the priority of manufacturing over agriculture and for accelerated industrialisation.

In their central ideological conflict, Trotsky defended his idea of "Permanent Revolution" against Stalin's theory of "Socialism in One Country".

Orwell believed that "Trotsky-Snowball was potentially as big a villain as Stalin-Napoleon, although he (Snowball) was Napoleon's victim. There is no certainty that as a dictator he would be preferable to Stalin, though undoubtedly he has a much more interesting mind".

The French Revolution and Napoleon Bonaparte

The French Revolution of 1789 was the first major revolution of modern times. Its ideals of liberty, equality and brotherhood were betrayed by Napoleon Bonaparte, who seized power in 1799, establishing himself as virtual dictator. A brilliant general and able administrator, he had a ruthless streak, but was not a mass murderer like Stalin ("Napoleon" of *Animal Farm*).

For Discussion

1. *Animal Farm,* in spite of its amusing surface, is actually a fable about some of the important problems which face mankind: Who shall rule a nation? How? By what authority? Can democracy work? Does power always corrupt?

2. It is manifestly an attack on Stalinism. It can be read as a lament for the fate of revolutions. But it is also

a profound and moving commentary on the circumstances of human life: each of us is forced to co-operate with others in order to get things done, but must compromise with his own truth and honesty in joint effort.

3. The film version gives to *Animal Farm* a happy ending. The animals all the world over, hearing how Napoleon has betrayed the animal cause, rise up against him at the end and, in a second revolution, expel him. After this second revolution, we are left to believe, a rule of freedom and equality is established and survives. But this ending makes nonsense of the whole thesis.

4. Orwell had defined the theme of this book. "History consists of a series of swindles, in which the masses are first lured into revolt by the promise of Utopia, and then, when they have done their job, enslaved over again by new masters."

5. *Animal Farm* was written to counter the widespread view that Socialism = Stalinism. Russia, as a war ally, was very popular in England, and Orwell hoped to immunise readers against potential disillusionment with socialism when Russian infamies came to light.

6. The plot of *Animal Farm* was not especially original. Kipling had written a story in the 1890's about "a yellow horse" who tried to rouse Vermont farm animals against "the Oppressor", man.

7. Some critics mistakenly talk of the overriding importance of the author's love of animals and fail to understand that Orwell, in *Animal Farm,* loves animals only as much or as little as he loves human beings. What is essential to the success of the satirical beast fable, is the author's "power to keep his reader conscious simultaneously of the human traits satirised and of the animals as animals".

8. The beast fable need not convey an optimistic moral, but it cannot portray complex individuals. The characters of a satirical animal story may be sly, vicious, cynical, pathetic, lovable, or intelligent, but they can only be seen as members of large social groups and not as individuals.

9. Communism is no more or less evil than Fascism or Capitalism — they are all illusions which are inevitably used by the pigs as a means of satisfying their greed and their lust for power. Religion, too, is merely a tool of the oppressors and a device to divert the minds of the sufferers.

10. *Animal Farm* remains powerful satire even as the specific historical events it mocked recede into the past, because the book's major concern is, not with these incidents, but with the essential horror of the human condition. There have been, are, and always will be pigs in every society, Orwell states, and they will always grab power. Even more cruel is the conclusion that *everyone* in the society, wittingly or unwittingly, contributes to the pigs' tyranny. Boxer, the noblest (though not the wisest) animal on the farm, devotes his unceasing labour to the pigs.

11. Frederick R. Karl, in *The Contemporary English Novel*, believes that *Animal Farm* fails as successful satire "by virtue of its predictability", but this terrifying predictability of the fate of all revolutions is just the point Orwell is trying to make. The grotesque end of the fable is not meant to shock the reader — indeed, chance and surprise are banished entirely from Orwell's world. The horror of *Animal Farm* is precisely the cold, orderly, predictable process by which decency, happiness, and hope are systematically and ruthlessly crushed.

SELECT BIBLIOGRAPHY

Books by George Orwell

Down and Out in Paris and London. 1933.
Burmese Days. 1934.
A Clergyman's Daughter. 1935.
Keep the Aspidistra Flying. 1936.
The Road to Wigan Pier. 1937.
Homage to Catalonia. 1938.
Coming Up for Air. 1939.
Inside the Whale. 1940.
Animal Farm. 1945.
Nineteen Eighty-Four. 1949.
Collected Essays, Journalism and Letters. 1968.

Books about George Orwell

Atkins, J. *George Orwell.* London: Calder, 1954.

Deutscher, I. *Heretics and Renegades.* London: Hamish Hamilton, 1955.

Eagleton, T. *Exiles and Emigres.* London: Chatto & Windus, 1970.

Greenblatt, S. J. *Three Modern Satirists.* New Haven: Yale University Press, 1965.

Hollis, C. *A Study of George Orwell.* London: Hollis & Carter, 1956.

Hopkinson, T. *George Orwell.* London: Longmans, 1953.

Wain, J. *Essays on Literature and Ideas.* London: Macmillan, 1963.

Williams, R. *Culture and Society,* Part 3, Ch. 6. London: Chatto & Windus, 1958.

Williams, R. *Orwell.* London: Fontana Books, 1971.

Woodcock, G. *The Crystal Spirit.* Boston: Little, Brown, 1966.